The Luxembourg House
on Beekman Place
Three Portraits in Time

By Debra Pickrel, Pamela Hanlon, and Marianne Matthews

First published in the United States of America in 2010 by
The Consulate General of Luxembourg in New York

GRAND DUCHY OF LUXEMBOURG
Ministry of Foreign Affairs

LE GOUVERNEMENT
DU GRAND-DUCHÉ DE LUXEMBOURG
Service information et presse

First edition, 2010

Design by Kathy McGilvery
Library of Congress Cataloging-in-Publication data is available from the publisher.

ISBN 978-0-615-35358-6-51995
Printed in the U.S.A. by Wentworth Printing

10 9 8 7 6 5 4 3 2 1

Table of Contents

Foreword

Welcome to the Luxembourg House, our country's home in New York City.

The grand duchy's presence in New York is one of many throughout the world. We have established these locations in surroundings that foster collaboration with other institutions and our local communities. These sites are centers of diplomatic, economic, and business meetings, as well as cultural events and other activities, creating a physical bond between nations. The Luxembourg House on Beekman Place is emblematic of these relationships.

Two decades ago, the Luxembourg government sought a place of prominence near the United Nations as the site of its Permanent Mission to the United Nations, Consulate General, Trade and Investment Office, and National Tourist Office. We felt an immediate synergy between the former residence of two distinguished American leaders, with its venerable past, and our country's future relationships.

This book portrays the three key periods of the residents' eighty-year history. I invite you to read about our treasured home's remarkable heritage, as well as how it is used today as a center for international outreach. While its function and surroundings may have changed over the years, the esteemed legacy of the Luxembourg House continues today, as a welcoming venue for our friends and colleagues.

— *François Knaff*
Consul General of Luxembourg in New York

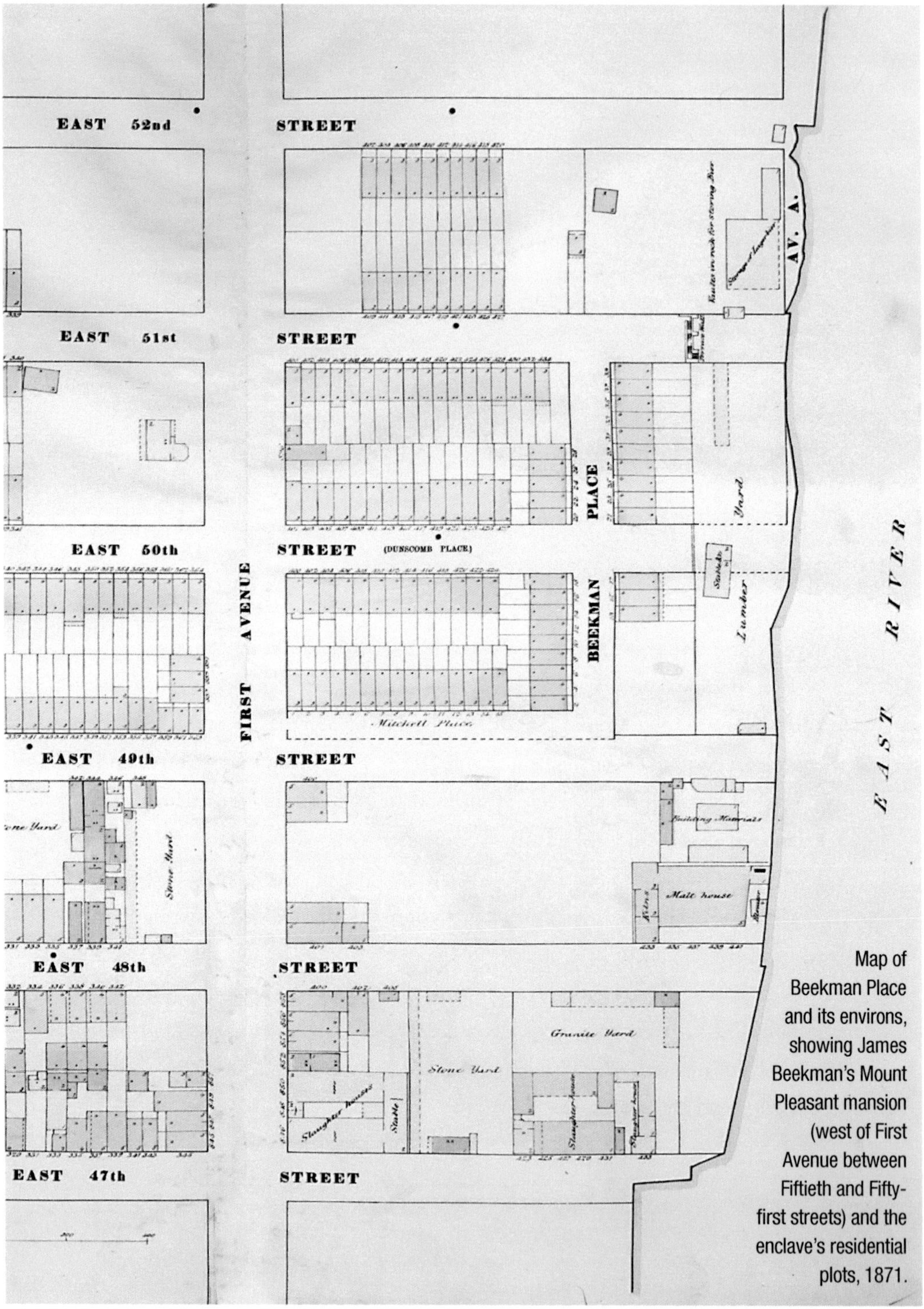

Map of Beekman Place and its environs, showing James Beekman's Mount Pleasant mansion (west of First Avenue between Fiftieth and Fifty-first streets) and the enclave's residential plots, 1871.

Prologue

The Elite Legacy of Beekman Place

The rocky bluff of Beekman Hill, rising above New York's East River in the neighborhood of Turtle Bay, is home to the rarified enclave of Beekman Place. Anchored by a street of the same name that marks its eastern boundary, this five-block residential area reaches west to First Avenue between Mitchell Place and Fifty-first Street. Once a verdant colonial estate, and later developed as the embodiment of refined living, it is today also dotted with foreign diplomatic missions and consulates. And 17 Beekman Place is among its most storied addresses.

The area that is home to Beekman Place was first settled in 1639, when the Deutal Bay Farm, reaching from what is now approximately Third Avenue to the river between Fortieth and Forty-ninth streets, was granted by the city's Dutch governor to two Englishmen. Beginning as early as 1712, these bucolic environs were referred to as "Turtle Bay," perhaps because of the "deutal" (knife blade) shape of the area's small bay or its prolific turtle population. Turtle Bay began

Lithograph of Manhattan's small Turtle Bay and its pastoral setting, 1858.

to play a key role in the city's burgeoning water transport and commerce business when a cargo wharf was added along its riverfront in 1734. In 1868, its little bay was filled in, the site of which is now covered by the United Nations' North Lawn, just south of Forty-eighth Street.

Beekman Place was carved from a section of the Beekman Farm, which lay north of the Deutal Bay Farm, extending to present-day Fifty-first Street. James Beekman, a prominent patriot and wealthy merchant descendant of an early Dutch settler, purchased the tract in 1763 and built his manor house, Mount Pleasant, there. Initially located near the intersection of what is now First Avenue and Fifty-first Street, his mansion was one of the grandest country seats in the city's early history. During the Revolutionary War, British Commander-in-Chief Sir William Howe commandeered it for his headquarters, and its greenhouse was the scene of the 1776 trial and sentencing of Nathan Hale as "a spy and traitor to the king."

Beekman died in 1837, leaving Mount Pleasant and its surrounding land to his nephew, James W. Beekman, a New York state senator and philanthropist. A few years later, when Fifty-first Street opened, the mansion was moved a block south, at great expense, to avoid its path.

In 1854, Beekman vacated Mount Pleasant after his wife contracted cholera. Conditions around the mansion were becoming increasingly swampy as construction of the city's 1811 street grid system moved north, and Europe—specifically, Switzerland—provided a healthier living environment.

While he was away, Beekman's property values escalated dramatically. Returning to New York in 1857, he moved into a townhouse at 5 East Thirty-fourth Street. From 1864 to 1866, as the days of rural estates waned in Manhattan, he began to sell off his highly desirable land to developers as small plots for private residences.

In 1865, Samuel W. Dunscomb, a former Methodist minister, acquired the property that would largely comprise Beekman Place. As a condition of purchase, he required Beekman to agree that neither

Lithograph of James Beekman's mansion, Mount Pleasant, which commanded views of the East River and the Turtle Bay, 1861.

he nor his "assigns" would ever construct buildings on their remaining riverfront property that would extend above the grade of Fiftieth Street—thereby blocking residents' water views—or that could be considered "dangerous, noxious or offensive" in any way. In return, Dunscomb erected a stone wall to uphold the embankment between his planned residential enclave and Beekman's residual holdings.

The intimate layout and single-family origins of Beekman Place are among its many distinctive qualities. Dunscomb developed the area with four-to-six-story brownstones, more affordable versions of New York's traditional marble or limestone-fronted row houses. Brownstone, a form of sandstone or freestone that weathers from pink to a dark brown over time, gained popularity in the 1840s as a building material used on the homes of the city's wealthy. According to early directories, original occupants of the enclave's brownstones held professional positions such as jeweler, doctor, and marble dealer.

Beekman Place's brownstones, looking north near the intersection of Fiftieth Street, 1910. Ellen Biddle Shipman purchased the brownstone on the northeast corner in 1919. The previous No. 17 is on the southeast corner.

Dunscomb lived in Mount Pleasant for a number of years after Beekman's departure. Destined for demolition, it was no longer listed in city tax assessment records by 1868. The grand mansion's 1874 demise marked the passing of an era.

James Beekman died in 1877, leaving half of his remaining property to his two sons and the other half in a trust for them to manage for their two sisters. Soon, the area along the bank of the East River began to deteriorate, bringing with it increased industrial development. Flanked by a coal yard to the south and an ice plant to the north, Beekman Place's aging brownstones degenerated into boarding houses. When Turtle Bay renewal began in the twentieth century, these residences were among the first to be rehabilitated.

In 1919, renowned landscape architect Ellen Biddle Shipman purchased 19 Beekman Place and converted it to a Georgian-style house comprising her residence, office, and two apartments. In 1922, the Beekman family decided to lease their remaining land—a strip along the waterfront and a plot at the south end of Beekman Place—following a prolonged attempt to break the Dunscomb restrictions so they

Waterfront view of a declining Beekman Place, looking northwest from Forty-ninth Street and the East River, 1905.

Ellen Biddle Shipman's Georgian-style residence at 19 Beekman Place precipitated the area's renaissance, 1926.

could develop it for commercial purposes. One Beekman Place, an opulent apartment building, as well as a low garage subleased by the Yellow Taxi Corporation, were constructed on their property. The Beekman Hill Association was formed around this time to oversee the area's transformation into a quiet and private domain of the elite.

Though abattoirs and factories still stood nearby, Beekman Place became an increasingly fashionable address during the 1920s and '30s. Its new and noteworthy buildings included the 1924 Venetian Gothic-inspired Beekman Terrace by Treanor & Fatio with J.E.R. Carpenter; the 1928 Panhellenic Tower, an art deco structure by John Mead Howells; and several other seminal high-rises. During this time, the area attracted a steady flow—and intriguing mix—of illustrious residents associated with literature, theater, and the arts, as well as government, business, and finance. Investment banker James V. Forrestal, who commissioned 17 Beekman Place as his elegant Manhattan residence, was among its celebrated newcomers.

— *Debra Pickrel*

Chapter One

The Forrestal Years 1929-1946

by Debra Pickrel

James Vincent Forrestal, who would later become the first United States Secretary of Defense, was a young Wall Street executive in 1929, enjoying his best of times in what would rapidly become the nation's worst. For nearly ten years before the stock market crash that fateful fall, New Yorkers had been busy flaunting the city's newly minted reputation as America's undisputed capital of the Jazz Age. This raucous decade of sophisticated frivolity and high-spirited spending blatantly mocked the somber restrictions of Prohibition. And the rich of the day had the most fun of all, living and playing in their chic Manhattan quarters or along nearby shores at their Long Island Gold Coast or New Jersey estates.

New York was the cash cow of the country during the Roaring Twenties, dominating the financial, legal, publishing, and advertising industries that were actively influencing consumerism, and Wall Street was the place to build a career and make a fortune. The booming economy fueled citywide construction, and iconic art deco skyscrapers burgeoned on the skyline. But the stock market's plummet on October

29, 1929, took with it all the inherent optimism of these dazzling days, ushering in the Great Depression. As the nation's largest city, New York was most affected by the crisis. By 1930, a quarter of its office space was vacant, homelessness was rampant, and people crowded the streets, selling anything to make money. By the end of 1932, nearly one in every four of its employable citizens was jobless. Nationally, the unemployment figure of four million at the end of 1929 more than tripled to thirteen million by 1933.

Flappers, young women who defied convention, personified the daring spirit of the Jazz Age, 1926.

Jim Forrestal was a rare exception in these unprecedented circumstances. A combination of his Wall Street firm's savvy business decisions, his own luck with some lucrative corporate deals, and his shrewd business acumen allowed him to survive the crash with his capital nearly intact. Such good fortune made the young investor one of the era's "golden boys."

Forrestal married *Vogue* staff member Josephine "Jo" Ogden Stovall in 1926, the year private residential construction began to decline in the city as property values in its most prized neighborhoods escalated. At the time, Jo was living at Beekman Mansion, a new ten-story Italian Gothic apartment building in the enclave of Beekman Place. Initially, the newlyweds lived in Forrestal's bachelor quarters at 32 Washington Square West, but after the birth of their first son, Michael, on November 26, 1927, more spacious accommodations were needed.

Perhaps influenced by Jo's affinity for the area, the Forrestals rented a townhouse at 27 Beekman Place. On June 4, 1928, they purchased 17 Beekman Place, located at the intersection of Fiftieth Street, with plans to demolish it for a new residence. A building permit was filed the following year. Forrestal viewed construction

Investors flood Wall Street following the 1929 stock market crash. The New York Stock Exchange (1903, George B. Post, architect) is on the right.

of this metropolitan home as a way to proclaim his professional standing and to elevate his social position, as well as that of his café society-loving wife. They could hardly have picked a better location, as the locale's prestige was growing by the day.

Seventeen Beekman Place was one of the last significant private residences built in Manhattan, all the more remarkable for its realization during the Great Depression.

An Ambitious Financier

Jim Forrestal was vice president of the preeminent investment banking firm Dillon, Read & Co. when he commissioned his Beekman

Forrestal as a Princeton University senior, class of 1915.

Place townhouse. Though still in his thirties, his net worth exceeded $5 million. But the young banker was not born on "Easy Street." In fact, he came from relatively humble beginnings.

Forrestal—often called "Vince" in his boyhood, and "Jim" later in life—was born in Matteawan (now Beacon), New York, on February 15, 1892. The last of three sons, he had a tolerant father—an Irish Catholic immigrant who owned a construction company—and a strict and punitive mother. While only about five feet eight at full adult height, the serious and inherently shy Vince Forrestal always had lofty ambitions. His father hoped he would take an interest in the family business, but he never did. His mother hoped that he would enter the priesthood, but her youngest grew to shun his religion as well as his modest origins, creating a lifelong gulf between them.

In high school, Forrestal was passionate about American history and English, and he demonstrated a natural aptitude for journalism. After his 1908 graduation, he worked as a reporter at a variety of area newspapers, then enrolled in Dartmouth College in 1911. One year later, he transferred to his dream school, Princeton University, where he would be more likely, he said, to meet "people who counted for something" in regard to his future aspirations in "newspaper work."

Less privileged than his wealthy classmates, he still managed to belong to the school's prestigious clubs and councils. His financial circumstances improved in his senior year, when he earned $1,200 as the outspoken editor of the campus newspaper, the *Daily Princetonian*.

Forrestal left Princeton just a few weeks before graduation for reasons that are not completely clear. He may have lacked a class credit from his Dartmouth transfer or failed a senior English class for missing lectures. Regardless, this dramatic fall from class leader to dropout was a shocking failure that Forrestal was determined to reverse.

After initial employment with the American Tobacco Company and the *New York World* newspaper, Forrestal made his way to Wall Street via a job in Albany as a bond salesman for William A. Read Company of New York (later Dillon, Read). During World War I, he enlisted in the Naval Reserve and trained as a naval aviator, achieving the rank of lieutenant junior grade. He received his discharge in December 1919.

The United States was a well-established world power after the war, and its largest city began attracting the most enterprising and creative minds from across the nation and Europe. Jim Forrestal was one of them. Returning to Dillon, Read, he rose rapidly in the company's ranks, becoming a partner in 1923, vice president in 1926, and president in 1938. His venerable career in the federal government would begin just two years later.

Forrestal was—and would remain—an enigma to most who knew him. He had a passion for power and wealth, but thought little of those who lived on inheritances or last name alone. Cynical about "society" and its related obligations, he knew it was crucial to his career to move in the proper circles.

A Social Butterfly

Josephine Ogden Forrestal was born in Chicago in 1900, the youngest of four children. Her father was a scholar and teacher from Fairmont, West Virginia, who became chairman of the state's Public Service Commission when Jo was young. He died when she was thirteen, and her mother moved the family back to Chicago.

Jo inherited a flair for style from her mother and a lifelong love of horses from her father. After high school, a defiant streak led her to elope, but she quickly divorced. Jo attended the University of Chicago, but she was more interested in the prospect of exciting romance and career opportunities than college. En route to Smith College, where her mother had arranged for her to finish her education, she stopped in New York to visit a love interest and never left the city.

Josephine Ogden Forrestal by renowned photographer Cecil Beaton, c. 1920s.

Establishing herself in glittering Manhattan, Jo became a chorus girl in the Ziegfeld Follies. One evening at a Ziegfeld party, she met Frank Crowninshield, editor of *Vanity Fair*. He hired her immediately to join the small staff of his magazine's sister publication, *Vogue*, where Jo's wit and irreverence won her a signature column. She was in her element, mixing and mingling with the city's crème-de-la-crème of fashion, society, and entertainment, always a stylish standout in the crowd.

It is believed that Jo initially met Jim Forrestal shortly after she arrived in New York, but in 1925, their paths crossed in a more meaningful way when both were on business trips in Paris. Jo became determined to marry her new love. Around the same time, she also realized that her career at *Vogue* was most likely in jeopardy, precipitated by her independent, elitist attitude—one that did not sit well with her editor. She would leave her position after becoming Mrs. James V. Forrestal. Jo and Jim married at Manhattan's Municipal Building on October 13, 1926, but, over time, they would lead largely independent lives.

An Exceptional Commission

In the late 1920s, Jim Forrestal made two significant real estate investments that would flaunt his achievements and reflect his social aspirations. He commissioned his luxurious residence at 17 Beekman Place, and purchased a thirty-acre country estate in Old Westbury on Long Island's North Shore that included The Old Brick, an 1820 manor house. These extravagant opportunities were possible for Forrestal on the brink of the Depression for three reasons. Clarence Dillon, the astute chief executive officer of Forrestal's firm, downsized his company from approximately seven hundred employees to one hundred following a March 1929 break in the stock market that he believed demonstrated uncertainty. Additionally, Forrestal reaped the rewards of a series of profitable business agreements with leading corporations, including the Goodyear Tire and Rubber Company and Dodge Brothers. Finally, he created a private Canadian company as a personal tax shelter.

Forrestal commissioned Harold Sterner, a young architect and artist who lived nearby, to design his Beekman Place home. A five-story residence was demolished to make way for the townhouse, and while it was under construction, other development hummed around it. Several luxury apartment buildings rose on the same block: the 1930 One Beekman Place, designed by Sloan & Robertson and Corbett, Harrison & MacMurray; and the 1931 Two Beekman Place, designed by renowned residential high-rise architect Rosario Candela. The city widened the street of Beekman Place at this time as well, replacing its granite block cobblestones with asphalt. The enclave's sidewalks were re-laid, accented by Bishop's Crook lampposts, and trees were relocated behind protective guardrails. It was into these exclusive environs that the Forrestals settled in 1932.

Seventeen Beekman Place is a five-story, Neo-Georgian, red brick townhouse of approximately 6,426 gross square feet (597 square meters) that rises from a cast-marble-clad ground floor. Built on a narrow 20-by-100-foot lot, Sterner maximized its street presence by positioning the main entrance on its long north facade, facing a square formed by the terminus point of Fiftieth Street. Set back fifteen feet from this street as well as from Beekman Place to the west, the building abuts a brownstone to the south. Its east facade, graced by a curved bay, faces the East River.

Harold Sterner, the Forrestals' Architect

Architect and artist Harold Sterner, who was in his mid-thirties when he received the Forrestal commission, lived close to Beekman Place at 346 East Fifty-first Street.

Harold Sterner, 1927.

Born in Paris on October 29, 1895, he was the son of noted portraitist and illustrator Albert, and his wife, Marie. Steeped in art from an early age, Sterner began painting in childhood without formal training. Choosing architecture as a career, he graduated from the Massachusetts Institute of Technology (M.I.T.) in 1917.

In 1923, Sterner married Leonie Clare Knoedler, daughter of Edmond L. Knoedler, a partner in a prominent Manhattan art gallery. The young couple was well connected and active in the New York and Long Island social scenes. Their only child, Michael Edmund, born in 1928, would go on to have a venerable diplomatic career.

Sterner worked for the Park Avenue architectural firm of Pennington & Lewis for a number of years. He was head designer and junior member there in 1926, when the firm gave 25-27 Beekman Place—two adjacent townhouses owned by diplomat, banker, and war hero Van Santvoord Merle-Smith—a $300,000 renovation including a Neo-Classical facade. The Forrestals subsequently rented No. 27, which is likely how Sterner and Forrestal met.

Architecture and art seemed equally appealing to Sterner. During the Depression, with business at an unprecedented low nationwide, he increasingly turned to painting and drawing to help support his family, focusing on ships, seascapes, and landscapes as primary subjects. The Forrestal commission was no doubt welcomed during this trying time.

The Forrestals' house was a prime example of 1930s residential architecture for America's affluent. Between the World Wars, a desire for renewed order and stability prompted a return to traditional styles, while a wish to embrace the future infused design with modern elements, producing eclectic results. Georgian architecture, derived from classical, Renaissance, and baroque forms, had been the country's prevailing style in the eighteenth century and was experiencing a revival. Simultaneously, the streamlined geometrics of art deco were

Like his prominent new client, Sterner had an inquiring mind, was obsessive and tireless in regard to his work, read voraciously, and was a history enthusiast. His passion for the sea led him to become an unofficial authority on historical marine design.

Though progressive, Sterner's architectural aesthetic was rooted in American tradition. Strong, clean lines with harmonious proportion and an exacting sense of style were his professional signature, attracting those with sophisticated tastes who sought originality not pushed to extremes. An expert draftsman, his renderings demonstrated a melding of accuracy and artistry—applied knowledge complemented by precise craftsmanship.

Sterner, who later practiced with architects Samuel Oxhandler and Musgrave Hyde as well as on his own, became best known for his domestic architecture, which numbered approximately twenty commissions. In addition to Forrestal, his other eminent residential clients included Averill Harriman, politician, businessman, and diplomat; and Samuel Lewisohn, art benefactor and founding trustee of the Museum of Modern Art.

Following a divorce, Sterner wed his second wife, stage and screen actress Paula Trueman, in 1935. From the early 1940s, exhibition sales of Sterner's paintings proved profitable, and he increasingly turned to art to make a living. Fantastical architecture was sometimes featured in his paintings.

In the mid-1940s, Sterner received a commission involving one of New York's most cherished landmarks. He remodeled Turtle Bay's Amster Yard at 211-215 East Forty-ninth Street between Second and Third avenues, a serene courtyard originally constructed around 1869 and presumed to be the terminus point of the Boston Stage Coach. Property owner James Amster hired Sterner to create a resource center for upscale homemakers that would house Amster's interior design firm as well as shops and offices for others. After the renovation, Sterner moved his home and office to the location. Amster Yard became a New York City Landmark in 1966.

Harold Sterner died in 1976 at the age of 80.

Beekman Place from East River Drive, 1940. The Forrestals' residence (center left) was constructed at the same time as the soaring One Beekman Place and Two Beekman Place (left, and behind it, center), and just after the Panhellenic Tower, which became Beekman Tower, a hotel, in 1934 (background, right of center).

ushering European modernism into American aesthetics. This push-pull of influences, past and present, was appealingly evident in the Forrestal residence.

Seventeen Beekman Place is topped by a copper mansard roof that envelops its fifth floor. Sterner reduced this floor in height a bit so the residence would not look like a "baby skyscraper" from the street, he said. The building's exterior is accented by brick pilasters with Ionic capitals, unadorned medallions, and cast-marble string coursing, which reflects the domination of horizontal lines over vertical in classical design. The upper string course has scroll detailing. The front door of the house, which originally had a medallion detail, is surmounted by a cobalt blue glass address marker and flanked by two Corinthian columns supporting a narrow architrave and french balcony. A second entry on Beekman Place was used by the Forrestals' servants, providing access to the main kitchen, the cellar, and a back hallway. The building is surrounded by an iron fence, behind which small trees were planted. A compact terrace garden adjacent to the east facade is enclosed by a red brick wall. Its herringbone-patterned brick surface with an octagonal

James V. Forrestal residence, 17 Beekman Place, 1945 (left). Classical urns embellish the iron fence (above).

central space is surrounded by lush plantings.

A diverse variety of windows, reflective of the Georgian style, enliven the house: traditional sash versions, the most dramatic of which reach floor-to-ceiling in the second floor living room overlooking the East River; Palladian sash designs on the north facade that feature ornamental grates; and french windows on the fifth floor that open outward. Two window apertures on the north facade—for bedrooms on the third and fourth floors—were created for symmetry, but were not initially cut through. A diminutive ocular window with a decorative grate is a charming detail that

fronted the entrance foyer's powder room.

The decorating firm of Jones & Erwin designed the interiors of the residence. Headquartered in New York, their offices were deco-modern with classical accents, a theme echoed in the Forrestals' house. There, aspects typical of the Georgian style, such as a central staircase, oval rooms, columns and pilasters, pine paneling, fan and herringbone-patterned floors, and classical cornices, were counterpointed by art deco elements such as a geometric marble floor and sunburst and sunray details. A creative mix of traditional and modern furnishings completed the eclectic setting. An urbane design publication of the 1930s described the decor of the house as "sensitive to the twentieth century character," noting its "repressed elegance" and "counseled understatement." "The whole house has style," it summarized.

A small vestibule led through an archway into the Forrestals' oval entrance foyer. Its gray marble floor featured a cube and black diamond pattern with a lighter gray and yellow-rose border, accented by a fan motif at each end. A graceful oval staircase against the far wall was the focal point of the space. Grand in statement rather than scale, it provided guests access to the second floor and the family access to the floors above.

The main entrance of 17 Beekman Place, showing the vestibule's marble floor (above). The ground floor's ocular window (below).

The foyer's walls were painted antique white to contrast with its marbleized pilasters, which were warm sienna with yellow accents. Gilded sconces on either side of the entranceway had snake arms encircling black Medusa head medallions. The curved paneled doors on the east side of the room opened into closets. Those on the west side opened into a powder room on the front of the house, and, at the rear, a custom-designed elevator that is still in operation today. The elevator could also be entered from the back hallway, providing entree to a fifth floor apartment suite when the rest of the house was closed for the summer season. Sliding entry doors and metal gates, a pine-paneled interior with a diamond-patterned ceiling,

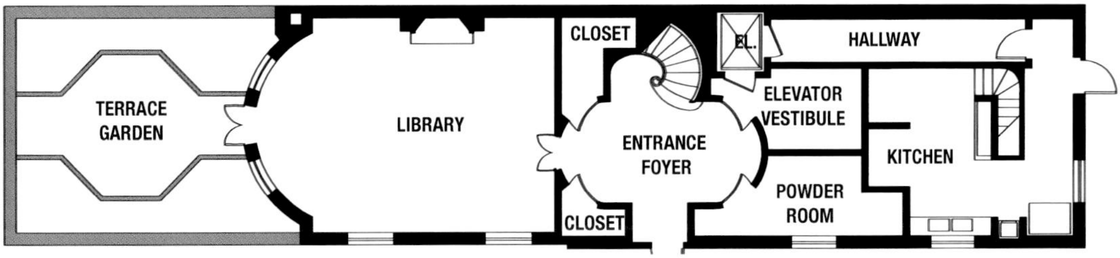

Ground floor

and golden sunray details contributed to the elevator's singular design.

Forrestal's favorite room in the house was the pine-paneled library east of the foyer. Ideal for conversing with male guests after dinner over brandy and cigars, it had a view of Welfare Island (now Roosevelt Island) and renowned architect James Renwick's 1854 Smallpox Hospital. The key focus of the library was its fireplace, which originally had a black marble surround and an elaborately carved mantel. French doors at the far end of the room opened onto the terrace garden.

The entrance foyer's eclectic decor (below) extends to its pine-paneled elevator with sunray details (bottom).

The second story of the house was designed for entertaining. It comprised a generous reception hall joining sophisticated yet refined living and dining rooms with herringbone-patterned floors. An oval colonnade of white Corinthian columns encircled the hall, complemented by a white ceiling, cornice, and doors. Beige walls were the backdrop to the pristine space, classic gilded sconces flanked the doors to the adjacent rooms, and a bas-relief frieze was positioned above the living room door. An antique green glazed statue of Pomona, Roman goddess of fruit trees, gardens, and orchards, stood in front of the central window, framed by white moiré draperies. The hall's parquet floor, crafted from two shades of walnut, featured a herringbone pattern radiat-

Second floor

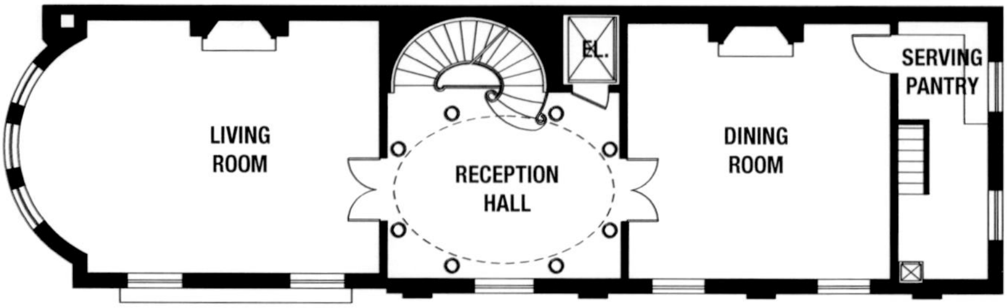

The second floor reception hall between the living and dining rooms was a gathering place for the Forrestals' many illustrious guests.

ing from the center of the space.

The walls of the airy living room on the second floor's east side were painted a cool "Robert Adam blue," according to the designers. Silver leaf adorned the room's acanthus-patterned cornice and highlighted a sunburst relief on the ceiling. White and off-white, as well as textural mixes, added subtle contrast in the space. Works by two twentieth-century painters, the Japanese/French artist Leonard Tsuguharu Foujita and Russia's Natalia Gontcharova complemented the understated palette. The door frame's pediment above egg-and-dart molding, the chair railing, and the classical marble fireplace mantel added formality to the room. The crowning attribute of the elegant space was its panoramic view.

The dining room, on the west side of the house, was painted a classic nineteenth-century blue found in the portrait above its fireplace, which was rendered in the style of Neo-Classical French painter, Jean-Auguste-Dominique Ingres. Gold leaf swathed the room's cornice and also accented the ceiling relief around the chandelier, mirrors, doors,

and fireplace surround. The dining table was antique white with a black marble top, its chairs upholstered in a red and white stripe. Red velvet drapes with gold fringe graced the windows, a nod to the attire of the woman in the portrait. A serving pantry adjacent to the dining room was accessed by a small stair from the kitchen, and a dumbwaiter aided food transport between the two.

The family's private quarters were on the third and fourth floors. Curved floor-to-ceiling display alcoves at the head of the stairs on each of these levels echoed the architectural sensibilities of the house. Underscoring Sterner's meticulous approach to design, they created small landings as well as decorating opportunities.

The dining room played host to frequent dinner parties. The paneled door in the corner leads to the serving pantry.

The third floor was "somewhat modernistic" compared with the public floors below, according to the architect. The centerpiece of Jo's chic circular bedroom, which overlooked the river, was an opulent bed with a sea scallop-shaped headboard. Her glamorous bathroom,

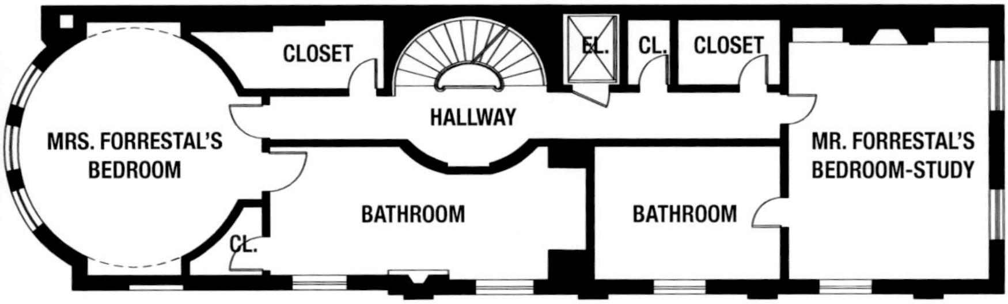

Third floor

Sumptuous details, including glistening decorative panels (right) and a harmonizing fireplace surround (below), defined Jo Forrestal's bathroom.

accessed through a door on the bedroom's west wall, had marble fixtures, a Lucite dressing table, and gilded sconces adorned with crystals. Reflective gold panels backpainted with classical designs decorated the room's upper perimeter as well as its fireplace surround.

Jim Forrestal's bedroom-study and bathroom were at the opposite end of the paneled hallway. His working and sleeping quarters were sleek yet simple, furnished much like a cabin on a luxury liner. The walls and floor of the room were cork. The floor was stained a dark, polished tobacco brown, and a cinnamon bear rug lay in front of the fireplace, which had a curved surround the color of polished steel. Zebra wood furnishings were complemented by a metal desk chair upholstered in honey-colored leather, as well as an arm chair. A single cabinet bed with a shelf and cupboard space ran along the wall, its coverlet a honey-

The decor of Forrestal's bedroom-study was luxurious yet austere. An interplay of texture and pattern defined the space.

colored corduroy. Waxed pine venetian blinds and cafe au lait silk damask curtains dressed the windows. Forrestal boxed in his youth in an effort to build his slight physique, and a favorite George Bellows lithograph portraying the sport hung over his desk. A piece by *New Yorker* cartoonist Peter Arno hung on the opposite wall.

Furnishings for work and sleep were in close proximity in Forrestal's bedroom-study.

The fourth floor of the residence included a nursery for the couple's two sons (their second son, Peter, was born on August 2, 1930), servants' quarters, and bathrooms. At their Long

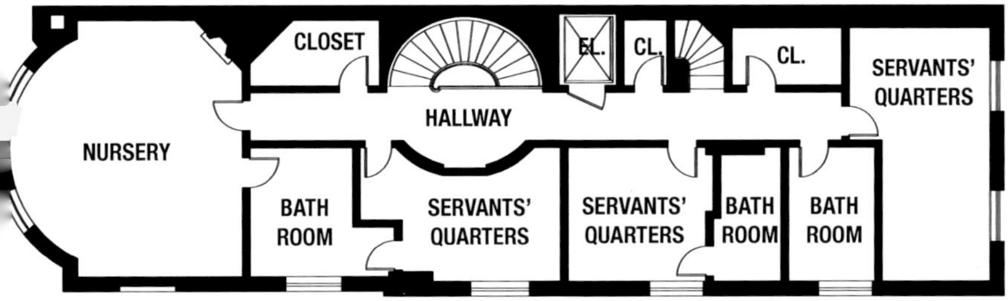

Fourth floor

Island estate, the Forrestals spared little expense when it came to domestic help, employing a chauffeur, cook, gardener, butler, valet for Jim, lady's maid for Jo, and a nanny, though not all of them lived with the family. A similar scenario was likely at 17 Beekman Place. A central calling system for servants at the house included a buzzer in each room and a main panel in the kitchen.

The fifth floor of the house, accessed via the elevator or a small wooden staircase from the fourth floor, was a separate apartment that could be used by guests. It comprised a bedroom on the west side of the house, a bathroom and kitchen along the central hall,

Fifth floor

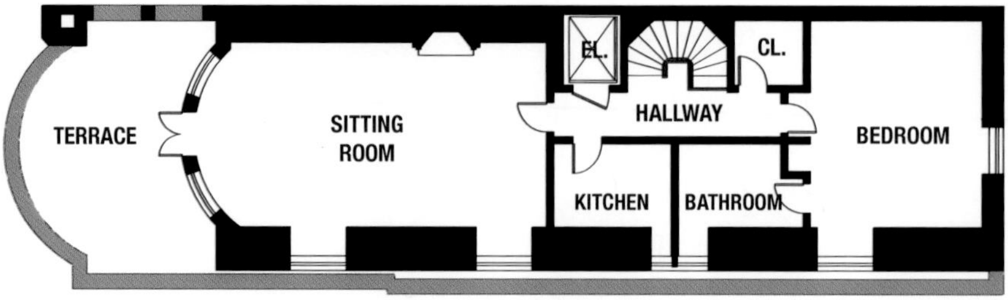

and a sitting room to the east that opened onto a brick apron terrace providing far-reaching views.

The fifth floor terrace offered expansive views of the East River, Roosevelt Island, and the borough of Queens beyond.

The Trappings of Success

Diana Vreeland, renowned editor-in-chief of *Vogue*, described Jo as "creative" and said she "knew how to make a house interesting." Seeking drama in her surroundings, Jo approached the finishing touches of decorating as a stage designer might, more concerned with "look" than authenticity. Many of the unlikely objets d'art at 17 Beekman Place were procured during her frequent trips to antique shops along Third Avenue, including the dining room portrait and the reception hall's Pomona statue. Forrestal appreciated his wife's entertaining acumen and flair for style, but teased her about her "theatrical eye" when it came to such decorative additions.

Accents with the patina of time may have been fine for her home, but Jo was meticulous about her fine wardrobe. As a former *Vogue* staff member and leading socialite of the day, she was a "fashion plate" with an image to uphold. Jo had a particular affinity for precious jewelry and frequented elite purveyors such as Seaman Schepps, known for his exuberant designs. Her husband was equally aware of the impact of his attire, insisting on custom-made suits, jackets, and slacks from Brooks Brothers or London's Anderson & Sheppard, shoes from Peal, and shirts from Beal & Inman.

The Forrestals' many social engagements provided plentiful opportunity to display their good taste. Surrounded by a host of famous neighbors, it is likely that the guest lists for their numerous cocktail and dinner parties included many of these luminaries.

The *New York Times* is peppered with references to the couple's comings and goings during their years on Beekman Place, both together and alone. They attended gala Newport dinners; foxhunts; horse shows; race meets; lunches with counts and countesses, society scions such as Mrs. Cornelius Vanderbilt Whitney, and Russian nobility such as Prince Serge Obolensky; as well as a host of benefit events. Perhaps their most extravagant affair was the 1934 Opera Ball, which attracted two thousand guests to view a glittering pageant set in the Louis XV era of French history. A cast of hundreds was dressed to represent members of the courts and former courts of France, Poland, Scotland, and Russia. Jo, playing a member of the Polish Court of Lunéville, France, danced the minuet. In 1935, the Forrestals gave a dinner in the Persian Room of the Plaza Hotel for actor Gary Cooper and his wife, attended by the Countess of Warwick; William Paley, president of Columbia Broadcasting System (CBS), and their Beekman Place neighbor; and famed photographer Cecil Beaton, for whom Jo was one of many enchanting subjects. In 1936, Jo and Jim, along with songwriter Cole Porter, spent the weekend with Hermann Oelrichs Jr. and his wife, Dorothy, at their spectacular Newport "cottage," Rosecliff.

Jo, who had a lifelong affinity for equestrian pursuits, frequented the Meadowbrook Hunt in Hempstead, Long Island, c. 1930s.

The Forrestals also traveled a great deal in the 1930s. In addition to springtime jaunts to Hobe Sound near Palm Beach, Florida, they frequently journeyed to Europe. Dillon, Read had offices in London and Paris, and Jo often accompanied her husband on trips there. While Forrestal worked constantly, Jo visited friends in St. Tropez or other chic locales.

The couple was dedicated to charitable causes, as well. Jim was a trustee of the National Foundation for Infantile Paralysis. His interest in the organization was likely related to his own serious bout with pneumonia as an infant, which left him frail as a child. Among the many worthy causes Jo supported was the Turtle Bay Music School at 244 East Fifty-second Street, which provided music education for children. Yet, she and her husband did not express a great deal of interest in their own boys.

In Good Company...Renowned Residents

No. 1 **David K. E. Bruce** – diplomat and author; and his wife, Ailsa Mellon, daughter of Gilded Age magnate and U.S. Secretary of the Treasury, Andrew W. Mellon

William J. Donovan – founder of the Office of Strategic Services, forerunner of the United States Central Intelligence Agency (CIA)

John P. Marquand – novelist and Pulitzer Prize winner for *The Late George Apley*

Mary McCarthy – novelist, memoirist, and critic

David Milton – lawyer with real estate and financial interests; and his wife, Abby Rockefeller, benefactor and daughter of philanthropist John D. Rockefeller, Jr.

John D. Rockefeller, III – philanthropist, brother of Abby Rockefeller

Archibald Roosevelt – son of President Theodore Roosevelt; distinguished army officer and commander of U.S. forces in World Wars I and II

Edith and Maude Wetmore – daughters of George Peabody Wetmore, governor of Rhode Island and United States senator; Edith was president of Newport's Old State House and a Fellow of the Metropolitan Museum; Maude was a Republican leader

No. 2 **Noel Coward** – English playwright, composer, director, actor, and singer

Helen Hokinson – celebrated *New Yorker* cartoonist

No. 18 **Russel Wright** – industrial, housewares, and furniture designer; and his sculptor wife, Mary; both lifestyle marketing pioneers

Sons in the Shadows

Michael Vincent and Peter Ogden Forrestal grew from ages five to thirteen and two to ten, respectively, during the time they lived on Beekman Place. Their father, who was stingy with time, money, and affection when it came to his sons, had just two goals for them—to be good athletes and to become self-reliant. While Forrestal was at least intermittently aware of his shortcomings as a father, he seemed

OF BEEKMAN PLACE IN THE 1920S AND '30S

No. 19-21 **Alfred Lunt and Lynn Fontanne** – legendary stage acting couple

Ellen Biddle Shipman – renowned landscape architect

No. 22 **Prince Alexis Obolensky** – Russian noble immigrant and vocal teacher; and his wife, Princess Luba Obolensky, Park Avenue dress shop proprietor; Prince Serge Trubetskoy, a Russian noble and student, was their boarder

No. 23 **Katharine Cornell** – "first lady of the American stage" who played Elizabeth Barrett in *The Barretts of Wimpole Street* on Broadway; and husband, Guthrie McClintic, stage director and producer

No. 29 **William B. Paley** – president of Columbia Broadcasting System (CBS); and his wife, Dorothy Hart Hearst, formerly married to John Randolph Hearst, third son of newspaper magnate William Randolph Hearst

No. 25-27 **Van Santvoord Merle-Smith** – diplomat, banker, and war hero; General Douglas MacArthur's executive intelligence officer

No. 33 **William B. Leeds** – son of Gilded Age mogul William Bateman Leeds, Sr., an owner of the American Tin Plate Company and often called "the tin-plate king"

Jackson E. Reynolds – chairman, First National Bank

Billy Rose – Broadway producer, Songwriter's Hall of Fame member (lyricist), and theater/nightclub owner

The Forrestal sons, Michael (left) and Peter, in the terrace garden with their cousin, Jean Stanard (later McKinley), Jo's niece, c. late 1930s.

powerless to alter the circumstances or change course.

Jo was only slightly more attentive to the boys than her husband, "receiving" them in the morning as she enjoyed breakfast in bed. The boys most often dined with the family's servants in New York, and they spent a great deal of time at the family's Long Island home, away from their parents. There, their father met with them in his library on Friday nights, when they reported to him about their week's activities, which included attending Episcopal Sunday school.

Forrestal was conscious of the extravagant life his family was leading while much of the country was unemployed and close to starvation. He wanted the boys to attend public school in Roslyn, a town adjoining Old Westbury, but Jo said they would be teased for being rich. So, he gave in and enrolled them at Old Westbury's Greenvale Academy, and he and Jo saw them on weekends.

When Michael was ten and Peter was seven, they were sent to school in Switzerland, but returned to New York following the outbreak of World War II. Eventually, Jo enrolled them in the Aiken School in South Carolina, which she learned about from her riding friends. A winter escape for wealthy Northerners and home to prestigious equestrian events, Forrestal thought the town would be too much like a resort, but Jo prevailed, and the boys were happy there. They were enrolled at the Aiken School when their father received an appointment from President

Roosevelt that would prompt him to leave his illustrious career—and New York—behind.

A Higher Calling in Washington, D.C.

The family lived at 17 Beekman Place until 1940. Early that year, Forrestal spent time with Harry Hopkins, one of Roosevelt's closest advisors. The United States' entry into the war in Europe seemed imminent, and Forrestal let Hopkins know he would welcome an opportunity to leave Wall Street for service in the government. In June, he was appointed one of six new administrative assistants to the president.

The Forrestals at the White House on the occasion of President Roosevelt's fourth inauguration, January 22, 1945. Forrestal was secretary of the navy at the time.

Forrestal's new position paid $10,000 a year, a mere fraction of his Wall Street earnings. Jo, anticipating her husband's drop in salary as well as the coming war, made the practical decision to sell the couple's Old Westbury estate and buy a farm in Dutchess County near Roosevelt's beloved Hyde Park home. The family moved out of their Beekman Place residence, and Forrestal assumed his job as a White House aide on June 29, 1940.

Forrestal quickly gained the respect of Roosevelt administration members, and on August 22, he was sworn in as under secretary of the navy, with the critical job of procuring urgently needed ships, planes, and munitions for the looming two-ocean war. Forrestal's intellect, organizational abilities, and financial skills served him well in the role, and he was widely credited as the driving force behind building the U.S. fleet into the largest and most powerful in the world. In 1944, he went on to become secretary of the navy, a cabinet position at the time. And in September 1947, after congress passed legislation to unify the armed forces, President Truman appointed Forrestal the country's first secretary of defense.

• • •

Finding it difficult to leave his prized New York home, Forrestal offered it for rent for several years following his departure. Daniel G. Arnstein, president and owner of the Terminal Transportation System, was one of its residents. During his time in Washington, Forrestal considered a return to private life on Beekman Place, writing to Arnstein that he "plan[ned] to take back the house that autumn [1945]" as his home. This surprised his tenant, who said he had previously received two letters from Jo expressing her intentions to "convert the house into a rooming house for paying guests." Neither prospect came to fruition. When Forrestal finally decided to sell the house the following year, he passed it on to another giant of his time, one of America's greatest songwriters.

Chapter Two

The Berlin Years 1947-1989

by Pamela Hanlon

PERHAPS IT WAS DESTINY THAT LED IRVING BERLIN TO the handsome house on Beekman Place overlooking the East River, the home where he would live for the last forty-two years of his 101-year life. Maybe it was simply a yearning to settle beside the river where, as a young boy, he learned to swim in the murky waters near his family's tenement on the crowded Lower East Side. It may have been the river's allure that his wife, Ellin, often talked about—the view in the morning light, the sound of the passing boats, the swirl of the tidal currents. For sure, he liked the house, with its seven fireplaces, wood-paneled library, and spacious sun-filled rooms, including a fifth floor sitting room where the prolific composer could work at his piano into the small hours of the morning. Berlin and Ellin had talked about owning a house in the city for years. This one was special. "Your father and I had our eye on this house for a long time," Ellin told her three daughters when they moved into 17 Beekman Place shortly before Christmas 1947.

Irving Berlin was the most popular songwriter of the century. By the late 1940s, he had published more than eight hundred songs and written musical scores for dozens of Broadway shows, revues, and Hollywood films. Since 1911, when he literally burst onto the international stage with his first big hit, "Alexander's Ragtime Band," Berlin had gone on to write such beloved standards as "Cheek to Cheek," "How Deep Is the Ocean," "Always," "Say It Isn't So," "A Pretty Girl is Like a Melody," and "White Christmas." During the two World Wars, his fund-raising revues for the army had the whole country humming his soldiers' "reveille" number, "Oh! How I Hate to Get Up in the Morning." And he had composed a song some suggested should be the new national anthem, "God Bless America." Berlin's contemporary, the composer Jerome Kern, famously declared: "Irving Berlin has no *place* in American music. He *is* American music."

In the fall of 1947, Berlin was enjoying some of the biggest triumphs of his career. His long-running musical *Annie Get Your Gun*, starring Ethel Merman, continued to thrill audiences on Broadway. It had recently opened in London and soon would be on the Paris stage as *Annie du Far West*. The movie *Blue Skies*, with an Academy Award-nominated number, "You Keep Coming Back Like a Song," was playing in motion picture theaters across the country. And in Hollywood, filming had just begun on what would be another Berlin screen hit, *Easter Parade*, starring Fred Astaire and Judy Garland.

With *Easter Parade* underway, Berlin had returned to New York and he and Ellin were planning the family's move to the red brick house on Beekman Place. For the Berlins, it would mean more than simply packing up and bringing their belongings from the family's Upper East Side apartment to Midtown. They had been married nearly twenty-two years. He was fifty-nine, she was forty-four, and their youngest daughter would be twelve on her next birthday. The worldly, celebrated couple was coming to their new house with rich and touching memories—remembrances of their childhoods, his amid poverty and hers amid opulence; their unlikely but happy marriage; the ever-intense spotlight on his fame; her budding success as a novelist; and the love for their three bright, spirited daughters, growing up fast. Within just a few weeks, the Beekman Place house would become a home—filled with comfortable furniture, family portraits, photographs, heirlooms, keepsakes, *and* pianos—reflecting the remarkable lives of the Irving Berlins.

For the library, Berlin would bring a favorite antique English oak tavern table from his bachelor days. His much-prized Moroccan leather-bound Shakespeare volumes would sit on the library shelves. Two tall paneled screens of Chinese painted leather, wall covering from Ellin's childhood home, would stand in the dining room. A delicate, life-sized portrait of Ellin, aged twenty, would be hung over the fireplace in Berlin's top floor sitting room. And a bold 1920s charcoal sketch of Berlin would go above the library fireplace.

In the living room on a small antique French table, Ellin would place an oval-framed photograph of her strikingly attractive mother, Katherine. And on an antique chinoiserie secretary-bookcase in the living room near the windows by the East River, Berlin would place a gold-framed photograph of his Russian immigrant mother, Leah. She and her husband, Moses, had brought their young son to America in 1893.

Soon, the unpacking done, the house on Beekman Place would begin to tell the story of the renowned composer and his family.

Growing Up on the Lower East Side

Irving Berlin, born Israel Beilin on May 11, 1888, was just five years old when his parents fled their small village in czarist Russia. With seven children, they made their way to New York, through Ellis Island (where the family name was inadvertently recorded as "Baline") and onto the teeming streets of the Lower East Side. There, in New York's poorest neighborhood, they settled into a small four-room apartment on the third floor of a packed tenement building at 330 Cherry Street.

"Izzy"—as Israel was called when he was a child—was a small, thin boy with curly black hair. The youngest in the family, he often sneaked out of the cramped apartment on hot summer nights to sleep on the fire escape or the roof. As soon as he was old enough, he got a job as a newsboy, selling the *New York Evening Journal* on street corners after school. And whenever he could, he ran off with the neighborhood kids to the docks at the foot of nearby Montgomery Street, where they swam in the chilly waters of the East River. Izzy got to be a good swimmer, sometimes making it all the way across to Brooklyn and back.

Irving Berlin at about the age of thirteen, in a photo thought to have been taken for his Bar Mitzvah.

"With me, as a kid, it was a case of doing what came naturally," he said years later. Not only swimming, but singing, too, seemed to come naturally for Izzy Baline. His father, a cantor back in Russia, worked in kosher meat markets on the Lower East Side. But he also sang in the choir at the local synagogue. It was there that Izzy, with his clear, boy's soprano voice, learned to sing along with his father. "It was in my blood," he said of his musical talents.

When his father died, Izzy, just turned thirteen, quit school to work as a newsboy full time. He soon left home, and found a series of odd jobs that brought him closer to the world of music. He worked as a busker, singing for pennies; as a song "plugger" at a music hall; and then, in his first real break, as a singing waiter at a saloon in the heart of Chinatown, a place called the Pelham Café. There, the handsome young man—still in his teens—sang and waited tables from eight in the evening until six in the morning for seven dollars a week, plus all the coins he could collect as he "passed the hat."

Before and after work, Izzy tinkered on an old upright piano in the back room of the Pelham, and it was there, in 1907, that he wrote the lyrics for his first published song, "Marie from Sunny

Italy." It was not a success, but it did give the songwriter a new name. When the sheet music came back from the printer, the lyricist's name had become "I. Berlin." From then on, Izzy Baline would start to go by the name of Irving Berlin.

The Pelham Café in Chinatown, where Berlin worked as a singing waiter and where, in 1907, he wrote the lyrics for his first song, "Marie from Sunny Italy."

Within a couple of years, he was working as a lyric writer for a Tin Pan Alley firm, turning out as many as five songs a week and soon writing both music and lyrics. With no training—he could not read or write music—he played only in the key of F sharp, known as the black-note key. "The black keys are easier on the fingers," he would say with a smile. Berlin soon bought a transposing piano—he called it his "trick" piano—which had a lever under its keyboard to shift the piano into other keys. Throughout his life, he worked on a trick piano, and it would be a trick piano that he would play in the fifth floor sitting room of his Beekman Place house.

In 1911, a mere four years after writing his first song, the syncopated beat of "Alexander's Ragtime Band" brought the young composer worldwide fame. In Berlin's words, it set "the heels and shoulders of all America and a good section of Europe to rocking." Soon, he was writing musical scores for Broadway, with such future standards as "Play a Simple Melody" and "I Love a Piano." After army service in World War I, during which he wrote the first of his fund-raising, morale-boosting revues for the troops, he was back in New York with his own music publishing house, Irving Berlin, Inc., and soon, with partner Sam Harris, his own theater on Broadway—the Music Box on West Forty-fifth Street.

Berlin at the piano in his office on Broadway, just a few years after his 1911 hit song, "Alexander's Ragtime Band," brought him worldwide fame. On the wall is a photograph of his friend and colleague, entertainer Al Jolson.

In 1925, at just thirty-seven, Berlin was considered so accomplished that his life story was published as a book, written by Alexander Woollcott, an influential drama critic. Woollcott described the extraordinary rise of the boy who came from a family "as poor as a family can be," recounting the personal side of Berlin, as well as the professional. He wrote of Berlin's buying his mother a rocking chair with his first meager royalties, and later, after the success of "Alexander's Ragtime Band," finding her a comfortable apartment in the Bronx. He wrote of the tragedy of Berlin's 1912 marriage, when his bride died from typhoid fever contracted on their Cuban honeymoon. It was a loss that left Berlin struggling for a time, writing songs that were, Woollcott wrote, "all limp and sorry." But when Berlin picked himself up, he went on to write a string of hits. By the time the biography was published, Berlin had a catalogue of more than three hundred songs. The most recent, a waltz called "What'll I Do," was selling faster than any song he had ever written. For Berlin, however, the song would be remembered for another reason. It would lead to a conversation with a beautiful young woman and the beginning of a lifelong love affair.

Meeting Ellin Mackay

Ellin Mackay was a socialite and heiress, the daughter of one of the wealthiest men in New York, Clarence Mackay. Her grandfather, John Mackay, had made the family fortune in silver mining on

Nevada's Comstock Lode. A willowy blonde with delicate features and a refined way of speaking, Ellin had grown up in a world far distant from Irving Berlin's life on the Lower East Side. Her home was a fifty-room Louis XIV-style mansion on 650 acres on the North Shore of Long Island. Ellin's mother and father had divorced when she was just ten years old, and her father, an ardent Catholic and ever-protective parent, raised his three children on the magnificent estate, called Harbor Hill, with its vast formal gardens, European sculpture and fountains, and well over 100 servants.

In May 1924, Ellin, then twenty-one years old, found herself at a Manhattan dinner party at which Irving Berlin was also a guest. Over dinner, she turned to the famous composer and, with her soft, slightly affected accent, she said, "Oh, Mr. Berlin, I do so like your song, 'What Shall I Do?'"

Ellin Mackay at about the time she and Berlin met in 1924.

In his clear, blunt voice, he replied that the title of the song was actually "*What'll* I Do?"

When she seemed somewhat taken aback, he added, amused, "Where grammar is concerned, I can always use a little help."

The conversation apparently went well from there, since when the dinner party ended, Berlin invited the young heiress to a nightclub in Greenwich Village. Soon, there were other dates—dining and dancing at the Astor Hotel roof, trips to Coney Island with friends, including Cole Porter, and then, when Ellin began to fear word of their romance would get back to her father, they began meeting in his bachelor's apartment, a richly decorated duplex on the top two floors of a distinctive six-story building he owned at 29 West Forty-sixth Street.

When her father heard about the encounters, he was enraged. He did not approve of his daughter seeing a man fifteen years her senior, not to mention the fact that Berlin was an immigrant Jew in the unseemly theater business. He forbade Ellin to see him, hired detectives to follow Berlin to try to uncover something disreputable in his life (they didn't), and finally sent her off to Europe for six months to let the whole affair cool down.

That didn't stop the couple from exchanging letters and cables, and two of Berlin's biggest hits of the time were said to have been inspired by Ellin's absence—"All Alone" *("All alone,/I'm so all alone;/ There is no one else but you.")* and "Remember" *("Remember the night,/ The night you said,/'I love you,'/Remember?").*

When she returned from Europe, her father sent her away again, a separation that moved Berlin to write what would be one of his all-time best selling songs, "Always" *("I'll be loving you/Always,/With a love that's true/Always.").*

On the morning of January 4, 1926—eighteen months after their chance encounter at the dinner party—Ellin Mackay and Irving Berlin met at his place, and then, to avoid reporters and photographers who

Berlin on Growing Up Poor

Just months before he moved to his elite Beekman Place address in 1947, Irving Berlin returned to his boyhood home on the Lower East Side with a newspaper reporter. When his Russian immigrant parents and their large family settled on Cherry Street in 1893, the neighborhood was the poorest, most crowded in the city. The street's mostly Jewish, Italian and Irish families were packed into narrow tenement buildings with small, cramped rooms and little or no plumbing, ventilation, heat or light.

Berlin remembered that in addition to his job as a newsboy, he made money for the family by selling off bits and pieces of his mother's old brass samovar that she had brought from Russia. "I'd get five and ten cents for the pieces and kept selling them until the entire samovar disappeared," he said.

"You never miss luxury until you've had it," he said of his days as a youngster. "I never felt poverty because I'd never known anything else."

"Everyone should have a Lower East Side in their lives," Berlin said.

might see them slipping into his limousine out front, took the subway downtown to the Municipal Building. There, in the presence of a judge, they were married.

The next morning, banner headlines streamed across front pages of virtually every New York newspaper with the "scandalous" news that the young heiress had married the famous songwriter from the Lower East Side against her father's wishes.

For the next five days, reporters and photographers followed the newlyweds' every move, until the couple boarded the S.S. *Leviathan*, settled into the presidential suite, and set sail for a six-month stay in Europe. There, the media frenzy only picked up again.

Ellin and Irving Berlin run from reporters and photographers after their elopement in January 1926.

Clarence Mackay, meanwhile, drew up a new will; Ellin was excluded from her inheritance. But she got a precious wedding gift from her husband. Berlin presented her with the song for which she had been the inspiration—the copyright, including all royalties, to "Always."

In August, the couple returned to New York and soon moved into their first Manhattan home together. It was Berlin's West Forty-sixth Street duplex, now redecorated to accommodate his bride's softer, feminine tastes. And the apartment included a nursery. On Thanksgiving Day, 1926, Ellin gave birth to their first child, Mary Ellin. The event was cause for another round of newspaper headlines, and the occasion for a new Berlin song, "Blue Skies," which he dedicated to his baby daughter. *("Blue Skies/Smiling at me/Nothing but blue skies/Do I see.")*

Decades later, long after their children had grown and the Berlins were living quietly on Beekman Place, some would wonder at the couple's seemingly secluded life in their later years. Recalling the intense publicity surrounding their marriage, Berlin said, "We had more press attention at that time than anyone could have wanted for a lifetime."

New Yorkers at Heart

The couple didn't stay in Berlin's bachelor pad for long. When in New York, they often lived in a suite at the Warwick, a new luxury hotel near Broadway that was popular with theater people. At the same time, Hollywood's burgeoning movie business, with its new "talkie" films, was beckoning. The couple and their young daughter spent much of their time on the West Coast. From time to time, they considered moving to California permanently. But the Berlins were New Yorkers at heart. "There's no Lindy's in Los Angeles. No paper at two in the morning. No Broadway. No *city*," he once told his wife. (Lindy's was a fabled delicatessen-restaurant near Times Square, frequented by the theater crowd.) And she observed, "Even the sun is backwards in California."

The Berlins aboard the S.S. *Ile de France*, summer 1929. They were returning to New York after a European holiday.

In 1930, Berlin and Ellin thought about building a house in Manhattan. They bought property on East Ninety-third Street, between Madison and Park Avenues, where they planned a five-story house, not unlike the one being built about the same time for James Forrestal and his wife at 17 Beekman Place. But, with the lingering effects of the 1929 stock market crash, Berlin decided it wasn't the time to invest in a big house.

Instead, the Berlins moved into a three-story penthouse apartment on East End Avenue at the corner of Eighty-sixth Street overlooking the East River. The triplex was large, with plenty of room for two more babies—Linda Louise, born in 1932, and Elizabeth Irving, in 1936. It soon became a gathering place for friends and family, including Clarence Mackay, who had reconciled with his daughter and son-in-law in the late 1920s. With its terrace facing the water, the home brought Berlin back to the East River he had loved as a child, albeit in a far more upscale neighborhood and with Berlin now at the height of his success.

In 1934, Berlin was on the cover of *Time* magazine with a story that marveled at how, in his twenty-fifth year as a songwriter, he was adapting to the "changing fashions." Indeed, it was Berlin's "Blue Skies" that Al Jolson sang in Hollywood's first full-length sound track film, *The Jazz Singer,* released in 1927. And he went on to write songs for such early musical movies as *Puttin' on the Ritz, Mammy*, and a picture literally filled with hit tunes, *Top Hat.*

Berlin rehearses with Fred Astaire and Ginger Rogers, stars of the 1935 hit movie, *Top Hat*, featuring such Berlin favorites as "Cheek to Cheek" and "Top Hat, White Tie and Tails."

When Berlin's "God Bless America" was introduced in the troubled pre-war autumn of 1938, the public's response to the song was so overwhelming that Berlin himself had to squelch suggestions it replace "The Star Spangled Banner" as the national anthem. Four years later, the country at war, the ever-patriotic Berlin produced a show to entertain the troops and raise money for the Army Emergency Relief Fund. Considered the biggest undertaking of his life, Berlin toured with *This Is the Army*, a spectacular revue some critics called the "best show of a generation," for the next three years, as it played at war fronts throughout the world.

Meanwhile, back in New York, the family moved from their East End Avenue triplex to a large townhouse on East Seventy-eighth Street near Lexington Avenue in 1939. Then three years later, to scale back during the war when Berlin's earnings were being donated to the army, they moved again, this time to a smaller apartment at the corner of Gracie Square and East End Avenue, once more near the East River. The Berlins' oldest daughter, Mary Ellin Barrett, in her mid-teens at the time, recalled how pleased they were to be back by the river. "When we were living in the house on Seventy-eighth Street, I remember everybody in the family saying, 'We miss the river.'"

Shortly after he returned from touring with *This Is the Army*, Berlin was working on songs for what would be the all-time greatest hit of his career—*Annie Get Your Gun*, starring the legendary Ethel Merman. For Berlin and Ellin, the time finally seemed right to buy a house in the city.

Even before the war the Berlins had admired 17 Beekman Place. When the Forrestals moved to Washington in 1940, they rented the house to tenants for several years, before deciding to sell it—about the time *Annie Get Your Gun* premiered on Broadway. The Berlins bought the house in the late spring of 1946 and, after a delay related to a tenant's lease and renovations to the house, they moved into their new home in December 1947.

A House Becomes a Home

Just days after the Berlins' arrival at 17 Beekman Place, the house started to take on the unique character of the famed composer and his family. With them, they brought three pianos; countless books, including Berlin's collection of rare editions, Ellin's favorite French novels, and plenty of biographies and youngsters' books; family portraits by some well-known painters of the times; photographs; French and English antiques; and some much-loved furniture from their previous homes.

Linda Emmet, the middle Berlin daughter, was fifteen when her family moved to the house. "The curving staircase…I thought it was so beautiful," she recalled of the first time she stepped inside her new home, "and I really liked the paneled library, opening out onto the garden overlooking the river."

But she also remembered that the house didn't have enough bookshelves. "Even with the big library and other built-in bookcases, the house still didn't have enough shelf space for our family," she said. "Books were a big part of our lives."

Indeed, one of the alterations the Berlins made to the house was to add more built-in bookshelves. They also brought a more open feeling to some of its rooms by converting the oval entrance foyer and second floor reception hall (which the Berlins called the landing) to rectangular spaces, removing the arched entryway and decorative pilasters in the foyer and Corinthian columns on the landing. They eliminated the ornate relief detailing at the center of the living and dining room ceilings, and replaced the chandeliers in both rooms with one chandelier above the landing.

The Berlins made two other changes to the house—one, distinctly his inspiration and the other, Ellin's sentimental modification.

Berlin installed a projection booth in the back of the library, on the west wall, so he could show movies to friends and colleagues. In the late 1940s, it was relatively common in Hollywood for people in the movie business to show films in their homes. In New York, it was rare. Mary Ellin recalled that when she brought friends to their new house, "They were usually most interested in the projection equipment. It was a big attraction," she said.

The other alteration was more aesthetic. At the time the Berlins bought the house, the Harbor Hill mansion where Ellin had grown up was about to be demolished. The Mackay family fortune had been lost in the 1929 stock market crash, her father had died in 1938, and now Ellin's brother, who inherited the huge estate, sold it to a developer for a suburban housing project. The interior of the mansion contained some magnificent fireplaces, with elaborate European mantels. Ellin arranged for one of them—a richly carved English mantel—to be brought to Beekman Place, where it replaced the original fireplace mantel in the dining room.

The new mantel joined other Harbor Hill pieces at Beekman Place, perhaps none so spectacular as the pair of tall seven-panel screens of Chinese painted leather that had been wall covering in the mansion. Ellin placed them in the dining room on either side of the Harbor Hill fireplace. Crimson silk damask draperies hung on the dining room's north windows. And on the Queen Anne dining table was another heirloom, an 1863 Tiffany sterling silver wine cooler that had belonged to Ellin's maternal great-grandfather, William R. Travers, a prominent New York investor and co-founder of the Saratoga Race Course. The centerpiece represented yet another strand of family history that helped tell the story of the new proprietors of 17 Beekman Place.

Paneled screens in the Berlins' Beekman Place dining room were of Chinese painted leather that had been wall covering in Ellin Berlin's childhood home, the Harbor Hill mansion on Long Island. The carved fireplace mantel also came from Harbor Hill.

But none of the furnishings would define the family of Irving Berlin better than their pianos. In the ground floor library, a Steinway upright with walnut finish was placed against the west wall near the fireplace. There, Berlin might play for his family, and—with a little cajoling—for dinner guests. The Berlin daughters practiced their piano lessons at the library piano, or upstairs at the grand piano that stood in the second floor living room. The ebony lacquer Steinway, a model called the "living room grand," had been part of the Berlin household since it was delivered from the Steinway factory to the family's East End Avenue address on Christmas Eve 1935. On the fifth floor, along the west wall in his sitting room, was Berlin's favorite piano, a dark wood upright, one of his legendary transposing "trick" pianos. It was at this piano that he worked on his music, often into the early morning hours when the lifelong insomniac was known to be his most creative. (Berlin explained his sleeping habits simply, "When I started as a singing waiter, I worked nights and got used to sleeping days." He said that even when he could fall asleep, he dreamed he couldn't.)

Ellin asked a friend, Anne Urquhart, an interior decorator with the design firm Smyth, Urquhart and Marckwald, to help plan the rooms in the new house. But the Berlins insisted that the furnishings reflect their own lives. "For the most part, our parents furnished the house with things from their past, both for sentimental reasons and because they saw no reason to throw things away just because they moved. They were practical," said Linda, adding with a laugh, "Our extravagant mother could be frugal as well."

Library Filled with Memories

The library was furnished with some comfortable pieces from Berlin's duplex, dating back to his days as a bachelor. Two armchairs, with slipcovers of deep-brown chintz, stood on either side of his eighteenth-century English tavern table on the north wall, and lamps made from carved ivory Japanese figures were placed on tables at either end of the room. The figures were just two of a number of Asian ivories Berlin had been collecting since early in his career. Two new sofas, covered to match the armchairs, stood facing each other on a dark green carpet in front of the fireplace, while yellow velvet drapes framed the windows. The library's bookcases were filled with Berlin's collection of rare editions, from his Shakespeare set to an eight-volume biography of Napoleon.

A focal point in the library was the charcoal sketch of Berlin that hung above the fireplace. Drawn in the 1920s by the illustrator Neysa McMein, a friend and member of the Algonquin Round Table, it had served as the frontispiece in Woollcott's 1925 biography of Berlin.

"Almost all the paintings in the house were family portraits," said

Mary Ellin, pointing out that, like most of the furniture, each piece of wall art had some sentimental or personal significance. On the library's north wall between the windows, there hung an etching of Ellin as a six-year-old girl, by the French portraitist Paul Cesar Helleu. And above the library piano was a colorful Haitian primitive painting that Berlin and Ellin purchased on a vacation to the island with their daughter Elizabeth. Later, the Haitian piece would be moved to Berlin's upstairs sitting room, to be replaced in the library with a portrait of Ellin's grandmother, Marie Louise Mackay, with whom Ellin had always felt a special bond. The painting, by the great nineteenth-century French painter Jean-Louis Ernest Meissonier, had been the subject of international headlines in the 1880s when the sometimes temperamental Mrs. Mackay, then living in Paris, was reported to be so unhappy with the famous artist's portrayal of her face and hands that she destroyed the valuable Meissonier, some said with a poker. Now, the perfectly intact painting hung over the Berlins' library piano.

On the second floor, the living room was decorated in soft tones of blue. Draperies of oyster white silk brocade blended with new sofas and chairs in oyster white upholstery with pale blue fringe. Central in the room, with its twelve-foot ceiling and classical cornice, were two Louis XVI blue damask-upholstered chairs that had once been in Ellin's Harbor Hill sitting room. They stood on either side of the small antique Louis XV table on which the photograph of Ellin's mother was placed. And on the secretary-bookcase were the gold-framed photograph of Berlin's mother and a photo of his paternal grandfather. While no photograph of Berlin's father existed, he did have his father's silver Kiddush wine cup. It was placed in the bookcase above his mother's photo, along with two of his Chinese ivory figures.

On the living room's north wall between the windows hung a portrait of a young Ellin by American artist Lydia Field Emmet, and to the right of the fireplace near the west wall was a French decorative interior painting by Walter Gay, one of the most prominent American artists in Paris in the early twentieth century and married to Ellin's great aunt on the Travers side of her family. Over the fireplace was an eighteenth-century Venetian mirror with a beveled border of cobalt blue glass. It was complemented by a pair of candlesticks with cobalt

A large portrait of Ellin Berlin's mother, by Giovanni Boldini, hung above the sofa in the Beekman Place living room, while a gold-framed photograph of Irving Berlin's mother was on the secretary-bookcase. The chairs in the foreground were from Ellin's childhood home.

blue hanging prisms that stood on the mantelshelf.

Bedrooms were on the third and fourth floors, with living quarters for the household staff on the fourth floor in the back. (The Berlins referred to the side of the house facing Beekman Place as the "back" and the side facing the river as the "front.") Ellin's room, decorated in pale pink, was the front room on the third floor, the same room that had been Jo Forrestal's bedroom when she lived there. Ellin's four-poster bed, from her Harbor Hill home, stood against the north wall, its soft cream-colored canopy and bedspread catching the morning sunlight coming in off the river. While she kept much of the dramatic décor of Jo's large bathroom, she did some remodeling to make way for bookshelves.

A 1920s charcoal sketch of Berlin, by illustrator Neysa McMein, hung above the library fireplace.

Linda's bedroom was also on the third floor, in the back. It was the room that had been James Forrestal's bedroom-study. The youngest in the family, Elizabeth, had the bedroom on the fourth floor in the front, the room that was once the Forrestal sons' nursery. Both girls' rooms were painted blue, Elizabeth's an intense shade to contrast with white furniture. Like her mother's room directly below, Elizabeth's bedroom overlooked the river, with the Franklin Delano Roosevelt Drive (called the East River Drive until 1945) running alongside it. Years later, Elizabeth Peters remembered how, as a young teenager, she was fascinated by the late-night sounds of traffic on the Drive. "I never minded the noise. I found it interesting...lots of squealing brakes," she recalled. Meanwhile, the oldest Berlin daughter, Mary Ellin, was twenty-one at the time her parents bought the house and soon was living on her own.

Five household staff members lived in the house. At the start, François was the family's chef ("He made the most wonderful Gateau St. Honore," remembered Linda of his cream-filled cake ringed in pastry puffs and caramel); Odette was the parlor maid; Fernand, the butler/valet; Margaret, the maid; and Janet Tennant, or "Tenny," the housekeeper. Tenny, from Scotland, would be a part of the Berlin household for some forty years. First hired as a nanny for Linda, she later cared for Elizabeth, and then went on to look after all three girls. When the Berlins were away, Tenny was in charge.

On the fifth floor were Berlin's sitting room, opening out onto the lofty terrace overlooking the river, and his bedroom facing the back. In the sitting room where his trick piano stood, Berlin arranged much of his English antique furniture from his bachelor duplex, including an oak gateleg table and a refectory table. And over the room's fireplace hung the life-sized portrait of Ellin wearing a white dress with a wide blue sash. She had sat for the portrait, by Russian artist Savely Sorine, when she was twenty—shortly before she and Berlin first met.

A portrait of Ellin Berlin when she was twenty years old, by Savely Sorine, was over the fireplace in Berlin's top floor sitting room.

Once the Berlins settled into the Beekman Place house, they rarely rearranged their furniture. But the daughters recalled that in the 1950s, their parents made one key adjustment. Ellin acquired a large and important portrait of her mother, Katherine Duer Mackay Blake, by the Italian artist Giovanni Boldini, celebrated for his vibrant, flowing style of painting. Now, the grand piano was moved from the living room to the landing under the crystal chandelier, and the painting of Ellin's mother—who had been so fond of Berlin and who had given her blessing to her daughter's marriage from the beginning—would bring a final elegant touch to the already stunning living room.

Entertaining at 17 Beekman Place

The living room at 17 Beekman Place wasn't *only* about elegance. On occasion the furniture was taken out, the rug came up, Alexander Haas set up his three-piece band on the landing, and the spacious formal room became a dance floor for the Berlin daughters and their friends. "My parents gave some *fantastic* parties for us," said Linda, who remembered the big house as the perfect spot for dinner dances.

The two youngest Berlin daughters, Elizabeth (left) and Linda, in the family's dining room before a fancy dress party in the 1950s. The Berlins gave many large parties for their daughters at the Beekman Place house.

A New Year's Eve party became a tradition. A small band played as up to fifty or sixty young people mingled in the library and throughout the second floor, which was set up with small tables for food and drinks until the living room was cleared for dancing. "My friends all loved the parties my parents gave for us," recalled Elizabeth, "The house looked so beautiful, and I think because the parties were on two floors they seemed more interesting than other parties we went to."

If Berlin and Ellin entertained large groups at Beekman Place, it was usually in honor of their daughters. One of the largest gatherings was in 1959, when some ninety guests attended a wedding reception at Beekman Place following Linda's marriage to Edouard Emmet. "But for their own friends, our parents preferred to entertain with small dinner parties for two or three other couples," said Linda.

Anna Crouse, the widow of Russel Crouse, the playwright who worked with Berlin on two Broadway shows, fondly remembered evenings at 17 Beekman Place. Decades later, she recalled, "It was a beautiful house, and large. But it didn't feel like a large house. It felt like a home."

Playwright and director Moss Hart, a longtime Berlin friend, and his wife, singer and actress Kitty Carlisle Hart, were frequent guests. Composer Harold Arlen came to dinner at Beekman Place, as did singer Rosemary Clooney and her husband, actor Jose Ferrer; playwright Robert Sherwood and his wife Madeline; columnist Irving Hoffman; writer Anita Loos; and producer Leland Hayward and his wife, the fashion icon Slim Hayward.

The Berlins served cocktails in the library before moving upstairs to the dining room for dinner and then to the living room for coffee. "If my father was showing a movie in the library after dinner, then they had coffee down there," Mary Ellin remembered.

Family Dinners at Home

When the Berlin family dined alone at home, the girls joined their parents in the library over cocktails beforehand. (Berlin might have a bourbon; Ellin, a martini.) "And my mother's miniature toy Manchester was always with us," said Linda, "I still remember that tiny dog—the size of a rat, really—snuggling between the cushions of the sofa next to my mother."

After dinner, Linda recalled, Berlin often took a walk. "He would announce, 'Well, I think I'll get a breath of fresh air,' and then he would walk over to Broadway, poke his head into the theaters to see what was going on, and then walk back, or maybe take a taxi."

Berlin and Ellin frequently went out to dinner in the years after they settled into Beekman Place, usually before or after the theater. In the 1950s, they were often seen in the Cub Room at the Stork Club, night spot of the city's powerful and glamorous; at the Colony, considered New York's most expensive restaurant; and at two good steakhouses on the West Side, Dinty Moore's and Gallagher's. They also dined at a French place, Copain, just a block from Beekman Place on First Avenue. And, of course, Lindy's near Times Square forever remained a favorite with Berlin.

Christmas was always a special occasion in the Berlin household. In 1963, the growing family gathered at 17 Beekman Place to celebrate the holiday. Left to right, back row: the Berlins' oldest daughter, Mary Ellin Barrett; Edouard Emmet; Marvin Barrett; Edmund Fisher; and the Berlins' youngest daughter, Elizabeth Peters. On the sofa: Ellin and Irving Berlin and their middle daughter, Linda Emmet, holding her daughter, Caroline. In front: the Barrett children—Mary Ellin, Elizabeth, Katherine, and Irving.

For the Berlin girls, Christmas at home—with its traditional holiday dinner—was a special occasion. "…the single most beautiful and exciting day of the year," Mary Ellin recalled in her poignant book of family memories, *Irving Berlin: A Daughter's Memoir*, published in 1994. As daughters of a Jewish father and Catholic mother, she and her sisters were raised "…not to be good Jews or good Catholics or good whatever you might care to cite, but to be good (or try to be) human beings," she wrote. The girls were taught about both religions, although Berlin, never religious, left it to his Catholic wife to handle the dual lessons.

For Berlin and Ellin, the Christmas season came with sad memories. Their second child, a boy named Irving Berlin, Jr., had died on Christmas Eve 1928 at just three weeks of age. Still, they were determined to make the holidays a particularly bright time of year for their daughters. At the Beekman Place house, the Christmas tree stood in the foyer, in the niche in front of the oval staircase. Always a tall, full tree, it was lavishly decorated with colorful ornaments and lights, and topped with a star. The tree shared the foyer with a menorah on a table by the front door.

Christmas dinner began with turtle soup, followed by roast turkey with puree of chestnuts, puree of turnips and potatoes, string beans, and plum pudding for dessert…or some years, maybe pumpkin pie, the daughters remembered. Berlin carved the turkey. "Our father prided himself on his carving skills," said Mary Ellin, "not only the Christmas turkey, but roast beef, leg of lamb, whatever…he was very good at it."

In fact, Berlin enjoyed cooking. At their summer place in the Catskills (the fifty-two-acre estate had been Berlin's Christmas gift to Ellin in 1938), he grilled steaks on an open fire, often steaks specially ordered from Dinty Moore's, or sometimes trout that he caught in the stream on the property. Chefs at well-known restaurants were not surprised to find Berlin coming into their kitchens for some serious on-site consulting. And at Beekman Place, François, the chef, happily let Berlin have the run of the ground floor kitchen whenever he wanted it—which was usually late at night. "If one of us arrived home late with friends or a date, it was not unusual to find our father in the kitchen, ready to offer up one of his midnight 'feasts,'" said Mary Ellin. Scrambled eggs with tomatoes and finely chopped onions were a favorite.

If Berlin was not in the kitchen when they came home, the girls might assume he was upstairs at his piano. There, sometime in the fall of 1949, he started work on the score for a new musical. Soon, the keys of his trick piano would be sounding melodies for a show to be named *Call Me Madam.*

The satirical musical, about the United States' first ambassador to the Grand Duchy of Luxembourg, would be a huge success for Berlin—winning four Tony Awards, including one for best musical score. Decades later, the show would remain in the spotlight, not only for its ever-popular tunes, but because of a fascinating twist of fate that led the government of Luxembourg to buy Berlin's home for its New York offices. The music of *Call Me Madam*, about to be born at 17 Beekman Place, would live on in its halls for many years to come.

The Making of *Call Me Madam*

In June 1949, when President Truman announced his surprising choice of Washington hostess Perle Mesta to be the first U.S. envoy to Luxembourg, Berlin—busy with a new Broadway show, *Miss Liberty*, and working on the screen version of *Annie Get Your Gun*—no doubt paid little attention to the news. But within just a few months, he would be hard at work on a musical immortalizing, in the words of one of the show's opening tunes, "The Hostess with the Mostes' on the Ball."

The lively, buxom fifty-nine-year-old Mesta was an Oklahoma-born widow and wealthy oil heiress who had made her name by giving lavish parties for some of the most powerful names in government. She had been a top fund-raiser for Truman during his 1948 election campaign, and so her posting to Luxembourg—Mesta would be only the third woman ever to hold such diplomatic status—was met with considerable skepticism.

About the time of Mesta's appointment, the playwright Howard Lindsay was with his friend *Annie Get Your Gun* star Ethel Merman when he read a *Time* magazine story about the Luxembourg posting—"An Oyster for Perle," *Time*'s headline read. "...I've got a wonderful idea for a show for you!" he told Merman.

With that, Lindsay and his partner Russel Crouse started work on what would eventually become *Call Me Madam.* Merman, thrilled with the songs Berlin had written for her in *Annie Get Your*

Gun, wanted him to write the score for the new show. And Berlin was pleased to have another opportunity to work with Merman, with her strong, powerful voice. "I love to write songs for Ethel," he said. "Give her a song and she'll make it sound good. Give her a good song and she'll make it sound great. And you'd better write her a good lyric, because when she sings the words, the guy in the last row of the balcony can hear every syllable."

Call Me Madam star Ethel Merman rehearses with Irving Berlin before the show's 1950 opening. The show is based on the story of Perle Mesta, the United States' first envoy to Luxembourg.

Berlin did profess to wondering if it was a good idea to be writing about a living person. "We weren't quite sure whether we'd get hung or shot or something," he said later.

That didn't stop him from outlining the show in a press interview in late December. During a vacation in Rome with Ellin and daughters, Linda and Elizabeth, Berlin laid out the details: "It will star Ethel Merman, as Mrs. Mesta…It will portray the experiences of an American hostess in Washington who is appointed minister to a mythical duchy."

Meanwhile, Mesta herself didn't know anything about the plans. A few days after Berlin's interview appeared in newspapers, she was at a luncheon when one of the guests told her what he had read. "I was so upset…I could hardly go on with my lunch," she later wrote. "The more I thought about it, the more worried I got, wondering what they were going to put in the play."

With Berlin and Merman working together on the heels of their tremendous *Annie Get Your Gun* success, expectations were high for *Call Me Madam*, its story set in a country called "Lichtenburg." Weeks before its New York opening, the show had the highest advance ticket sales of any musical in Broadway history.

But after previews opened in New Haven, Connecticut, the show was in trouble. The first act had some good numbers, but, as Berlin later recalled, "There was a big hole in the second act."

Berlin retreated to his suite in New Haven's Taft Hotel to come up with a fresh, new number, leaving the cast and writers waiting anxiously. The story often told was that scriptwriter Crouse's hotel room was directly above Berlin's, and throughout the night, he could hear the loud tinkling of Berlin's piano through the floor. The next morning, Crouse rushed into the theater with a progress report, "I think he's got something. I keep hearing the same tune over and over!"

Stars Ethel Merman and Russel Nype on stage singing *Call Me Madam*'s biggest hit song, "You're Just in Love."

Indeed, Berlin did have something. And when he sang it for the writers and cast, Merman's reaction was simply, "We'll never get offstage."

That, in fact, almost happened. The song was incorporated into previews in Boston a few days later and the audience applauded for encore after encore of the new song, a lively counterpoint duet for Merman and co-star Russell Nype, called "You're Just in Love" *("I hear singing and there's no one there;/I smell blossoms and the trees are bare;"…"You don't need analyzing;/It is not so surprising").*

When *Call Me Madam* debuted on Broadway on October 12, 1950, the critics raved. *New York Times* critic Brooks Atkinson called the music one of Berlin's "most enchanting scores." And of Berlin's last-minute creation in a New Haven hotel suite, he said it "throws a little stardust around the theater and sets the audience to roaring."

Call Me Madam played on Broadway for eighteen months, went on national tour and a long run in London, and later was made into a movie. "You're Just in Love" stayed at the top of the music charts for months, something the sixty-two-year-old Berlin found particularly gratifying. "It's nice after all these years to know that you can still reach up there and find it when you're in trouble," he said.

Meanwhile, the "real" Perle Mesta kept up with news of the rave reviews, taking it all in stride. "I was really flattered by all the attention," Mesta said later, but she recalled that many people,

The Berlins and the Scouts

When the Berlins lived on Beekman Place, it was not uncommon to see groups of Girl Scouts in their khaki green uniforms making their way up the pretty tree-lined street to No. 17. Ellin, for many years a board member and vice president of the Girl Scout Council of Greater New York, hosted scores of young Scouts and their leaders, who regularly came to the house for conversation, and for tea.

Surrounded by Girl Scouts in the Berlins' Beekman Place living room in the 1950s are Ellin Berlin (left), vice president of the Girl Scouts Council of Greater New York, and Harriet Phipps, president.

Ellin's involvement with the Scouts dated back to 1940, when Irving Berlin set up a trust fund to distribute royalties from his patriotic song, "God Bless America," to the Girl and Boy Scouts of New York. The song had become so popular after it was introduced on Armistice Day in 1938 that Berlin felt its profits should go to charity. He and Ellin chose the Scouts so that young people in the city's poorer neighborhoods would benefit. He subsequently served on the board of the Boy Scouts for many years.

To date, the trust fund, called the God Bless America Fund, has distributed more than $10 million to the Scouts, and continues to benefit the Scouts each time the song is performed.

including Berlin, remained sensitive to her reaction. While *Call Me Madam* was still playing, she was at a dinner party at which Berlin and Ellin were also guests. "All through dinner, the talk was about his music," she said. "I noticed everyone carefully avoided mentioning his current hit. ...Just before the dessert course, I asked...in a loud voice, 'Isn't anyone going to talk about *my* play?'"

That brought an uproarious laugh, she said, and the rest of the evening was devoted to chatter about *Call Me Madam*.

Mesta's good humor and charm went a long way toward winning over her critics, and the hearts of Luxembourgers as well. She was an unconventional diplomat, for sure, but Luxembourg came to admire her energy and enthusiasm, her good connections in Washington, and, of course, her link to *Call Me Madam* and Irving Berlin.

From Broadway to Hollywood and Back

While Berlin was having a triumphant run on Broadway, his Hollywood films were drawing crowds as well. Shortly after the Berlins bought the Beekman Place house in 1946, *Blue Skies* opened in movie theaters around the country, starring Bing Crosby and Fred Astaire. *Easter Parade*, with Astaire and Judy Garland, was released two years later, introducing seven new Berlin songs, including "Steppin' Out with My Baby" and "It Only Happens When I Dance with You." In 1950, the screen version of *Annie Get Your Gun* was released, followed by *Call Me Madam* in 1953.

Two new Berlin movies premiered the next year—*There's No Business Like Show Business*, once again starring Ethel Merman and featuring Marilyn Monroe, and *White Christmas*, with Bing Crosby singing the Oscar-nominated tune, "Count Your Blessings Instead of Sheep." The song for which the film is named—"White Christmas"—was a holdover from an earlier Berlin movie, *Holiday Inn*. The song had won Berlin an Academy Award in 1943. Now featured in the film by the same name, "White Christmas" continued to have enormous audience appeal. "A publishing business in and of itself," Berlin once commented about the beloved holiday tune.

"White Christmas" also would find its way to the walls of 17 Beekman Place. In 1954, the year the movie was released, Grandma Moses, the popular folk artist known for her scenes of rural life in America, put the music to her palette, with her depiction of "sleigh bells in the snow," "treetops glistening," and "children listening." She called it *White Christmas*. Berlin liked the painting so much he wanted to buy it. "I chased it all over the world. Literally. It was going to one exhibition after another," he said. "I never seemed to be able to pin it down to acquire it."

When he finally did track it down, he hung the Grandma Moses scene of snowy country life in his office for a while, before bringing it home to Beekman Place. There, he put it over his trick piano in his sitting room. "She painted into that all that I wanted to say in 'White Christmas,'" Berlin said.

While Berlin worked at his trick piano, Ellin, in her third floor bedroom, was creating her own compositions. She was a prolific writer, whose articles appeared in the *New Yorker* and short stories in the *Saturday Evening Post*. In the mid-1950s, she was finishing up her most recent book, *Silver Platter*, a fictionalized biography of her grandmother, Mrs. Mackay. Published by Doubleday, it was the third of four novels she would write, and it stayed on the best seller list for weeks. "She wrote at home on her bed, in long hand on yellow legal pads," said Linda.

The daughters were proud of their mother's novels. "When I was very young, I always thought of her only as being a mother," remembered Linda, "When I realized her novels were published, I was very impressed!"

Berlin was proud of Ellin's writing too. He wrote a song to celebrate *Silver Platter*'s publication in 1957. Copyrighted but never published, the song ends: *"I'll give you on a silver platter/A*

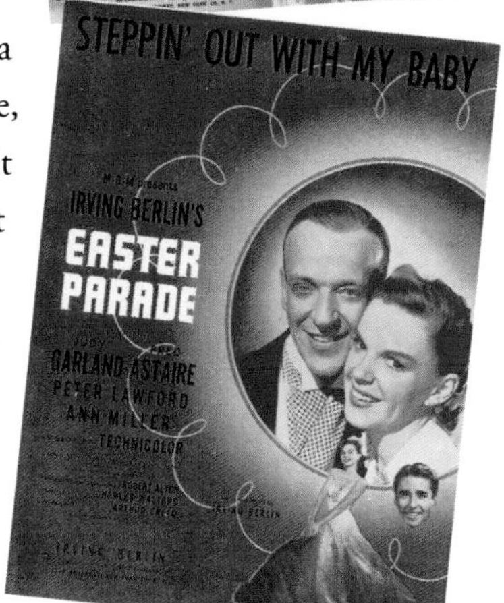

dream come true,/On a silver platter/With my love to you."

Berlin turned sixty-nine the month he wrote the tribute to Ellin's book, and he was beginning to worry about his age. He disliked the idea of getting old, of retiring. He began to fight bouts of severe depression from time to time, and he wrote little music for

Presidential Tributes

The Berlins enjoy a moment with President Eisenhower, as he presents Berlin with the Congressional Gold Medal in 1955.

During his lifetime, virtually every president from the 1940s paid tribute to Irving Berlin. For the unabashed patriot—forever grateful for the opportunities he'd been given since coming to America as a poor immigrant boy—three honors were particularly noteworthy.

At the end of World War II, President Truman awarded Berlin the Medal of Merit for his "extraordinary service to the United States Army" in creating and producing *This Is the Army,* an all-soldier revue that raised some $10 million for the Army Emergency Relief Fund. Berlin himself had toured with the show for three years, as it played throughout the United States, Europe, North Africa, the South Pacific, and the Philippines.

Later, Berlin was awarded the nation's two highest civilian honors. In a 1955 ceremony in Washington, President Eisenhower presented him with the Congressional Gold Medal, recognizing his many patriotic songs, including "God Bless America." And in 1977, President Ford honored Berlin with the Medal of Freedom. At nearly ninety, Berlin was not able to travel to Washington for the White House ceremony. Instead, a representative of the president came to 17 Beekman Place, where Berlin was presented the medal in a quiet, intimate ceremony in the library, with Ellin at his side.

the next several years. Then, in 1962 at the age of seventy-four, he wrote another musical score for the theater, again with scriptwriters Lindsay and Crouse. Expectations were high when the new show, *Mr. President,* premiered as a benefit at the National Theater in Washington, with President Kennedy and First Lady Jacqueline Kennedy heading a star-studded attendees' list. It was sold out for its entire two-and-a-half week run in Washington. The reviews were tepid, however, and it came to Broadway for a relatively short seven months.

First Lady Jacqueline Kennedy with Berlin at the Washington opening of *Mr. President*, September 1962.

Still, Berlin had another big musical stage triumph coming his way. In 1966, twenty years after it first opened on Broadway, Richard Rodgers produced a revival of Berlin's *Annie Get Your Gun.* As in the original, it starred Ethel Merman. Berlin wrote a new number for the show called "An Old Fashioned Wedding." A hit typical of Berlin's earlier days, the song literally stopped the show. At the Lincoln Center premiere, the audience called for *five* encores. Rodgers, in the back of the theater, was heard to say, "Not bad for a man seventy-eight years old."

Pondering *East River* in Later Years

Berlin continued to write songs for many years, and in fact, wrote his last known lyric less than two years before he died. He often thought about doing another musical, especially one about the East River, set on the Lower East Side of his childhood days. Of his upscale Beekman Place address, Berlin said, "I'm a little farther uptown, but we see the same tugboats and ships."

"I have nursed one idea maybe ten years. I have researched it, used my personal memories, and have written songs," Berlin said in 1966, shortly before the opening of the *Annie Get Your Gun* revival.

"I'd like to call it *East River*...a turn-of-the-century musical based on the immigrants, the already established Irish, the incoming Jews and Italians, their problems, triumphs, loves and disasters."

But Berlin would never write *East River*, or another stage or movie production. He saw the world transitioning to a younger generation. "Everything changed. The world was a different place. The death of President Kennedy, the Vietnam War, the social protest. Music changed too," he told music historian Robert Kimball, who along with Berlin's daughter Linda compiled *The Complete Lyrics of Irving Berlin*, published in 2001. "The Beatles and other groups reached audiences I couldn't," he said.

Berlin in the Beekman Place library in the early 1960s. Note the charcoal portrait of the songwriter above the fireplace.

Berlin started to spend more time at his artist's easel. Shortly after moving to Beekman Place, Berlin had taken up oil painting as a hobby. His only other leisure pursuit, aside from poker in his younger days, was fishing, usually in the stream at his Catskills summer place. Friends suggested he needed something more artistically challenging. So his "trick" piano was joined in his upstairs sitting room by an easel and oil pigments, set up near the windows overlooking the river. There, Berlin worked on still-life paintings and portraits, eventually cluttering his "studio" with his finished works. If he was happy with a portrait of someone he knew, he might give it to them. Barbra Streisand and Bing Crosby were among those said to have received their portraits. But Berlin knew where his real talents lay. "As a painter, I'm a pretty good songwriter," he was fond of saying.

In 1968, to mark his eightieth birthday, Berlin took part in a tribute, a ninety-minute television special of *The Ed Sullivan Show* on CBS. Some of the best talent in the country performed Berlin's greatest songs and attracted one of Sullivan's biggest audiences. Bing Crosby, Bob Hope, Robert Goulet, and Diana Ross and the Supremes performed, and Ethel Merman brought down the house with a medley from *Annie Get Your Gun*. Berlin sat in the audience with his family until the end, and then went onstage to sing "God Bless America," before a cake with eighty candles was brought out. Later, Berlin and Ellin, with their daughters and their families, gathered back at Beekman Place, in the library, for a smaller, quieter birthday celebration.

The Berlins as 'Grandpa' and 'Granny'

Over the years, Berlin and Ellin took pleasure in their roles as "grandpa" and "granny," entertaining their nine grandchildren at Beekman Place and, in the summertime, at their Catskills place. Ellin took her grandchildren to museums or the theater and as she had with her own children, she was forever encouraging them to read books. Berlin was filled with questions for his grandchildren—what were they studying, what movies were they seeing, what music were they listening to. Once, when his grandson Irving Barrett told him he was even more famous than the Beatles, Berlin was so amused he gave the youngster a $100 bill. His granddaughter Elizabeth (Mary Ellin Barrett's oldest daughter) recounted in her mother's memoir, "He pinched cheeks, literally, and told us girls we were smart and pretty." She said she thought her grandfather "seemed younger than some of the other grandparents I knew."

But Berlin did not handle aging with ease. When a reporter called to interview him for what became an annual ritual of Berlin birthday articles, Berlin told him, "For a guy who keeps having birthdays, it becomes damn boring."

Berlin continued to go to his office, in West Midtown, well into his late eighties. When he could no longer do so, he ran his business from Beekman Place. He stayed in close touch with old friends and colleagues by telephone, from phones in the library and his sitting room. "I'm in pretty good shape from the neck up," he would say. Among those with whom he reminisced almost daily was Harold Arlen, a friend since the 1930s. When Arlen was ill with Parkinson's disease, and Berlin was in his mid-nineties, Berlin would call to cheer him up, "Turn on CBS"—or NBC or whatever—"hurry, they're playing one of your songs."

Berlin took walks in the neighborhood in his later years, often with a nurse by his side. Doormen along the two blocks of Beekman Place remembered that he greeted them with his familiar quick, staccato voice as he passed by their buildings. On a mid-December morning, the doorman at 30 Beekman wished him a "Merry Christmas," to which Berlin quipped, "If I make it 'til then."

One neighbor, cabaret singer and songwriter John Wallowitch, frequently walked his dog along Beekman Place, and he and Berlin would nod to one another as they passed. But the encounter Wallowitch always talked about occurred on Christmas Eve 1983, when Berlin was ninety-five. Wallowitch and a small group of friends, talented musicians all, gathered at the corner in front of 17 Beekman Place and sang "White Christmas," then "Always," and then "White Christmas" again. The house was dark. Then, as they were about to leave, lights throughout the house lit up and a housekeeper invited them in. "Mr. Berlin would like to thank you," she said.

"We were simply astonished," said Wallowitch, "Here we were face-to-face with the greatest composer of our lifetime in his own house! He greeted us with his big bright eyes and shook hands with each of the guys and hugged the gals. 'Thank you,' he said, 'That was the nicest Christmas present I ever had.'"

Berlin's one-hundredth birthday, on May 11, 1988, was celebrated with a benefit performance at Carnegie Hall, on a stage of giant gold and silver piano keys arranged in ribbons and bows. Some two dozen performers—from Frank Sinatra, to Tony Bennett, to Willie Nelson, Marilyn Horne, and Leonard Bernstein—took part in the gala tribute that was broadcast two weeks later on CBS television. Before an illustrious audience including the three Berlin daughters and their families, honored guests sitting fourth row center, Walter Cronkite opened the evening. "... Irving Berlin helped write the story of this country by capturing the best of who we are and the dreams that shape our lives. Wander through his music, and you stand in wide-eyed amazement, that from the hand of one man could have glowed so much that is dear to us," he said.

Ellin and Irving Berlin in the terrace garden outside their Beekman Place library, fall 1969.

The honoree wasn't at Carnegie Hall that night. He was at home on Beekman Place. Berlin was now frail, and Ellin had suffered a stroke just weeks before. The couple marked his one-hundredth birthday quietly, alone together with dinner on trays in the pine-paneled library that had brought them so much pleasure over the years. It was a familiar room, filled with memories that had been a part of the house since the day they moved in. Still hanging over the fireplace, just as it had for more than forty years, was the sketch of a young Berlin in his thirties. Berlin's English antique tavern table still stood on the wall to the north. Over it, as always, was the pretty French etching of Ellin as a small girl. Berlin's leather-bound Shakespeare volumes remained on the library's shelves. His projection booth, not used for years, still stood at the back wall. And out front, the small terrace garden, as ever, overlooked the comings and goings on the East River.

Less than three months later, Ellin, Berlin's wife of sixty-two years, suffered another stroke and died at Doctor's Hospital on the Upper East Side. She was eighty-five. Berlin lived on for more than a year. On the afternoon of Friday, September 22, 1989, he died in his sleep at the age of 101, in his beloved home at 17 Beekman Place. He was buried next to Ellin at Woodlawn Cemetery in the Bronx.

• • •

On a mild December day four years after his death, Irving Berlin's three daughters and their families gathered back at 17 Beekman Place. There, on the side of the house between the two library windows—just steps from the East River that had been dear to their father since boyhood—a distinctive gray stone plaque was unveiled. It reads: "Irving Berlin (1888-1989) lived in this house for his last forty-two years."

Plaque on the facade of 17 Beekman Place.

The words are a humble but touching tribute to the man whose lifetime of work gave the world more than one thousand songs, music that has become a part of the very fabric of our culture—our history, our holidays, our homes, and our hearts—melodies that will live on...*Always.*

GRAND-DUCHE
DE
LUXEMBOURG

Chapter Three

The Luxembourg Years 1990-present

by Marianne Matthews

On April 30, 1990, the Grand Duchy of Luxembourg purchased 17 Beekman Place as the home for its New York City headquarters. Reflecting back on that day, Mary Ellin Barrett, eldest daughter of Irving Berlin, said, "We were all so pleased. It seemed like such a wonderfully completed circle that 17 Beekman Place, the home of the composer of *Call Me Madam*, was being bought by the Luxembourg government. ...This seemed to me just a very fitting finish to the history of the house."

The purchase of the house in light of the legacy of *Call Me Madam*, Berlin's highly successful musical about the United States' first female minister to Luxembourg, continues to be a topic of conversation, as well as a source of amusement and delight, for all those who now work at or visit what has become known as the Luxembourg House. The country's acquisition of the illustrious address also marked an exciting start to the next chapter of its life.

Just as the Forrestals and the Berlins used the house for entertaining guests, 17 Beekman Place today welcomes everyone from dignitaries to businesspeople to citizens and guests. While it serves as a home-away-from-home for Luxembourgers living in the New York area, its door is always open to New Yorkers and all Americans.

Discovering a Treasure

In 1989, the Luxembourg government launched its search for a New York City property. Michel Franck, a Luxembourg architect residing and working in the city as principal of Michel Franck Architect, was brought in on the project from the start. Working closely with Egide Thein, then consul general of Luxembourg in New York, the two scouted the East Side neighborhood of Turtle Bay for an appropriate location.

17 Beekman Place, 1991. The two blocked windows on the north facade were cut through during the conversion renovations by Michel Franck Architect.

"We did studies of several houses, always looking at the structure and the possibility of turning it into what the government needed," said Franck, presently managing principal at Spacesmith. "The Luxembourg government had specific requirements. For example, the house needed to be a place that could accommodate offices, but special events as well." Ultimately, 17 Beekman Place was selected for its prime location and the fact that the house was particularly well suited to the government's specifications.

At the time, the project team was unaware that the building had a Luxembourg connection. Thein simply talked with the agent and told him he preferred this particular townhouse. "He called me back the next day and told me a famous man had lived there and had died two months earlier," Thein told the *New York Times* several years after the purchase.

Following Luxembourg's purchase, 17 Beekman Place underwent restoration and renovation to convert the building to government use. The Luxembourg government appreciated the architectural and cultural treasure it had acquired and wanted to achieve an effective conversion, while preserving the building's unique character and heritage.

Michel Franck, AIA, managing principal, Spacesmith, led the renovation.

Franck, who had lived in New York for nearly a decade, led the restoration/renovation with a small team of designers and architects. "It was an important project from a business perspective, but it was also personally significant to me, as I viewed it as a contribution to both of my communities," he said.

According to Franck, the challenges for the team were both technical and aesthetic. Now that the house would be categorized as a "community facility" by the New York City Department of Buildings, the team needed to bring it up to the present-day building code while maintaining its character. This meant integrating mechanical systems such as air conditioning and plumbing, as well as safety systems including a sprinkler system, fire-rated doors and walls, and a smoke exhaust system—all without disturbing the inherent charm of the setting.

The team from Michel Franck Architect brought with them a depth of architectural expertise and creative solutions. They developed an innovative means of installing sprinklers without breaking the original crown moldings. Air conditioning ducts were concealed in the ceiling. The cellar was further excavated to ensure a second means of egress from the furnace room via a stairway that leads to the terrace garden. The building was brought up to code while maintaining the aesthetic feel of the original townhouse.

Projection booth apertures from the Berlin era on the pine-paneled library's west wall. During the Luxembourg government's renovation, the projection booth was removed to enlarge the foyer.

On the first floor, Berlin's projection booth was removed to expand the foyer. The powder

room was removed as well. The kitchen was converted into office space and bathrooms. In the library, the original pine paneling, which was damaged, was replaced by new mahogany paneling.

The architectural firm did not change the layout of the second floor. The goal was to preserve the space and its beauty, so that special events could be held here. The plaster moldings, both fireplaces—including the elaborately carved dining room mantel from Ellin Berlin's childhood home—the serving pantry, and a stairway to the kitchen were all maintained. The Luxembourg government even purchased the second floor landing chandelier from the Berlin family, which remains in place today.

Major renovations were made on the third and fourth floors, converting former bedrooms into offices. The fifth floor layout did not change, but rooms including the bathroom, the kitchen, and the closet were modernized.

While few changes were made to the exterior of the building, the original windows were single pane glass, and their gates were rusted. Both were replaced throughout the house with new ones that have a similar aesthetic to the originals. In addition, a new, more secure front door and one ocular window were installed. The ocular window, positioned on the right side of the main entrance, mimicked Sterner's original one that fronted the powder room and another that had been added just left of the entrance, fronting the Berlins' projection booth. Placed in a new niche space, the third ocular window brought light into the entrance hall and added a decorative touch.

The original single pane Georgian windows (top). An exquisite chandelier (center) and a fireplace mantel stained to a darker finish during the renovation (below) are among the decorative elements from the Berlin era that remain in place today.

Recalling how he and his team felt at the time, Franck said, "We were very proud the government of Luxembourg was interested in honoring this property. It was a very exciting project. We did it for the neighborhood, for the city of New York, and as a contribution to the Luxembourg community in New York City."

Under One Roof

The Luxembourg House opened its doors on September 9, 1993. Today, 17 Beekman Place is bustling with activity—from international business meetings to industry-specific functions, from commemorative occasions to cultural events. It is home to multiple and diverse entities of the country's government including the original Luxembourg Permanent Mission to

Grand Duchy Holds Grand Opening

On September 30, 1993, H.R.H. Crown Prince Henri, Luxembourg Minister of Foreign Affairs Jacques F. Poos, and Consul General Egide Thein held an official opening ceremony of the Luxembourg House, formally declaring 17 Beekman Place the new home of the offices of the Luxembourg Permanent Mission to the UN, the Consulate General of Luxembourg, the Board of Economic Development (later known as the Trade and Investment Office), and the Luxembourg Tourist Office. Some 250 guests including dignitaries from New York State and the City of New York attended the inauguration.

H.R.H. Crown Prince Henri of Luxembourg (center) with Egide Thein, consul general (left) and Jacques F. Poos, minister of foreign affairs, at the inaugural ceremony in 1993.

In his remarks at the ceremony, the crown prince congratulated all of those involved in the planning and restoration project. Regarding 17 Beekman Place, he said, "Luxembourg is honored to reside at a distinguished New York address. We are dedicated to preserving this historic building for other generations."

Poos noted the townhouse's unique connection to the grand duchy. "Our country has a deep sense of history, and we are delighted that our government is located in a classic American structure that has a link to Luxembourg thanks to the genius of Irving Berlin."

Today, diplomatic and business meetings, as well as social gatherings, take place in the library.

STATE OF NEW YORK
EXECUTIVE CHAMBER
ALBANY 12224

MARIO M. CUOMO
GOVERNOR

September 29, 1993

Dear Consul General Thein:

On behalf of the people of New York State, it is my great pleasure to extend our warmest greetings to His Royal Highness Crown Prince Henri of Luxembourg and His Excellency Mr. Jacques F. Poos.

We rejoice with you on the opening of the Luxembourg House, a site rich in historic and emotional significance for the people of both our nations. It is our hope that Irving Berlin's former home will serve as the focus for strengthening the ties of cooperation and friendship between Luxembourg and the State of New York.

Sincerely,

Mario M. Cuomo

The Honorable Egide Thein
Consul General and Trade Commissioner
Consulate General of
The Grand-Duchy of Luxembourg
801 Second Avenue
New York, New York 10017

the United Nations, the Consulate General of Luxembourg, the Board of Economic Development (later changed to the Trade and Investment Office, or TIO), and the Luxembourg National Tourist Office, as well as the more recent addition of the Luxembourg American Chamber of Commerce (LACC).

These entities work autonomously and also in harmony—all under one roof. Their overarching objective is to educate and promote the unique value and beauty of contemporary Luxembourg as a desirable destination for American business ventures as well as individual travel and exploration. In essence, their goal is to build progressive Luxembourg-American partnerships.

The former living room on the second floor is now used for conferences, formal dining receptions, and cultural events.

The Luxembourg House also serves as a comfortable haven for Luxembourg citizens who currently reside in and around New York City or who visit Manhattan. Finally, the activities of the house provide an inviting and compelling way for Americans to learn about the richness and vitality of modern Luxembourg.

A Sense of Harmony

Step inside 17 Beekman Place today, and you immediately experience its tradition of elegance and a sense of welcoming warmth. One cannot miss the foyer's centerpiece: the winding and stunning staircase that immediately invites the visitor to learn more about this historic venue. But before ascending it, let us pause to visit the ground level first.

The ground floor library still plays host to gatherings of businesspeople, dignitaries, and other guests. The room also plays a role in the many events that take place in the former residence. The terrace garden that brought so many years of enjoyment to the Forrestals and Berlins remains an outdoor extension to the activities and meetings in the library.

Climb the sweeping staircase to the second floor, which remains a gathering place for invitees who attend diplomatic working sessions, business breakfast seminars sponsored by the LACC, corporate meetings spearheaded by the TIO, a wide array of cultural events and exhibitions, and social receptions. The serving pantry, now the main kitchen, still serves its original purpose in facilitating entertaining in the house. The former living room now functions as event and conference space, its original fireplace, acanthus leaf molding, and appealing alcove windows in place even now.

A December Dedication

Irving Berlin will forever be remembered for his classic, "White Christmas." So it was quite fitting that the Grand Duchy of Luxembourg chose a wintry evening to remember the inimitable songwriter by placing a plaque in his honor at 17 Beekman Place.

On December 14, 1993, amidst nearly two hundred guests, a dedication ceremony took place in front of the five-story townhouse. A special plaque, carved by the stonecutters of the Episcopal Cathedral of St. John the Divine, was unveiled as a permanent tribute to Berlin and his many prolific years as an artist and resident at 17 Beekman Place. The year 1993 coincidentally marked the one-hundredth anniversary of Berlin's arrival in America from Russia.

Left to right: Berlin daughters Mary Ellin Barrett, Elizabeth Peters, and Linda Emmet, along with New York City Commissioner of Parks and Recreation Betsy Gotbaum, 1993.

All three Berlin daughters—Mary Ellin Barrett, Linda Emmett, and Elizabeth Peters—were in attendance. Other special guests included former New York City Mayor John Lindsay and performer Russell Nype, who catapulted his way to stardom in Berlin's 1950 Broadway musical comedy *Call Me Madam*.

A beautifully lit Christmas tree stood outside, surrounded by student singers from the Juilliard School performing excerpts from *Call Me Madam* as well as "White Christmas." The December dedication by the grand duchy to America's greatest songwriter will forever be embedded in history and the archival records of the Luxembourg House.

No, that is not the striking of Berlin's piano keys that resonates from the floors above. But they are good vibrations, nonetheless. The sounds that emanate today from the third, fourth, and fifth floors include the tapping of computer keyboards, the ringing of phones, and the ongoing auditory effects of the Internet. In short, it is the buzz of business being accomplished in the twenty-first century. It is here that the numerous personnel that comprise the Permanent Mission to the UN, the Consulate, the TIO, the Office of Tourism, and the LACC work toward their individual objectives as well as collaborate on specific initiatives. Irving Berlin would likely be pleased to see them working in perfect harmony.

Luxembourg City's old town and fortifications have been classified as a UNESCO World Heritage site since 1994.

Charismatic Personalities, Rich Roots

The Luxembourg House has long attracted charismatic personalities. If the walls could talk, one might hear the Forrestals hosting a lively dinner party or Berlin captivating a colleague with one of his newly composed songs. Today, the dialogue is among diplomats and dignitaries who gather there. Visits from ambassadors and heads of state are not uncommon.

While Berlin immortalized Perle Mesta, she was the first in a growing line of American women who have served as envoys to Luxembourg. Recent examples include Ann Wagner, who was appointed U.S. ambassador to Luxembourg by President George W. Bush in 2005, and Cynthia Stroum, who was appointed her successor in the summer of 2009 by President Barrack Obama.

Even as 17 Beekman Place has played a storied role in American history in these ways, the townhouse is now steeped in the rich roots of the grand duchy as well.

Luxembourg is often referred to as a land of many castles. In 963 AD, the first structure of a Luxembourgish nation emerged. Siegfried I of the Ardennes traded some of his ancestral lands with St.

Maximin Abbey in Trier for the remains of an ancient Roman fort. He built a "little fortress"—Lucilinburhuc—on the rocky summit and marked the location of a town destined to be a center of a new principality. A long line of Siegfried's descendants followed, but Gilbert, who ruled from approximately 1047 to 1059, was the first of his line to be denoted the Count of Luxembourg in the records.

Luxembourg remained an independent state in the Holy Roman Empire for some four hundred years. In 1310, when he was just fourteen years old, John the Blind became the Count of Luxembourg and significantly expanded the territory of Luxembourg through his many conquests. In *Cultural Guide to Luxembourg*, published in 2005 by the Luxembourg Ministry of Culture, Higher Education and Research, René Feis writes, "...he endowed his territory with an impressive network of castles whose lords swore allegiance to him and were then given their castles back in fief, owing feudal allegiance and service to him, thus becoming his vassals. This was the apogee of the feudal era in our area."

Vianden Castle, perched on a hilltop and overlooking the River Our, dates back to the eleventh century and is a popular tourist attraction today.

In 1354, history took another dramatic turn. John the Blind's son—Holy Roman Emperor Charles IV—elevated the status of Luxembourg to a duchy.

During the 1400s, Luxembourg fell under the rule of other empires—first Burgundy and then Habsburg. In the mid-1500s, the Spanish dominated the duchy. Later, the French invaded the territory and tried to lay claim to the land, but never fully succeeded. "France took Luxembourg City by conquest in 1684; France gave Luxembourg back to Spain by negotiation in 1698," writes James Newcomer in *The Grand Duchy of Luxembourg*.

After the War of the Spanish Succession, "Austria raised its flag over Luxembourg," states Newcomer. In 1715, the country was integrated into the Austrian Netherlands, and historians view the next eighty-year period as a good epoch for Luxembourg. The country enjoyed steady economic improvement, saw no wars, and the circumstances of daily life were better than those of the previous century.

The Gëlle Fra, which means "Golden Lady," is a monument that symbolizes peace and patriotism. It is situated on Constitution Square in Luxembourg City.

But peace did not last forever. French troops invaded, and in 1795, Luxembourg once again found itself under French rule. The duchy became a French *département,* and France imposed a totally new government. It was only after the defeat of Napoleon that Luxembourg's destiny became clear. In 1815, the Congress of Vienna gave formal autonomy to Luxembourg. The country was designated a grand duchy and William I, king of the Netherlands, became its first grand duke.

While Luxembourg continued to experience changes, the country remains a grand duchy today. After World War II, Luxembourg joined the new UN, and, in 1949, it became a founding member of NATO as well.

The current grand duke, Henri, became head of state in 2000 following the abdication of his father, Jean, at the age of seventy-nine. The grand duke and his wife, Grand Duchess Maria Teresa, have five children.

H.R.H. Grand Duchess Maria Teresa of Luxembourg (front, second from right) received the Path to Peace Award 2006 from the UN and visited the Luxembourg House.

Today, the population of Luxembourg is about a half million; the country is approximately the size of the state of Rhode Island; and it is situated where France, Germany, and Belgium meet. Given these circumstances, the Luxembourg spirit is one of openness, integration, and a keen awareness that the country's future is tied to innovation and mutually beneficial partnerships. This philosophy extends to 17 Beekman Place, where diplomatic, economic, and tourism initiatives foster successful collaborations and unite two great nations.

At Home and Away

Some of the most challenging work that takes place at the Luxembourg House is that of the Luxembourg Permanent Mission to the United Nations. While the ambassador, who serves as permanent representative of Luxembourg to the UN, and his or her staff maintain offices at 17 Beekman Place, their work extends well beyond this distinguished New York locale, crossing borders and impacting countries on every continent.

Ambassador Jean-Marc Hoscheit, permanent representative of Luxembourg to the UN (2003-2008), addresses an audience at the UN in 2008.

A multicultural and multilingual state in regard to its history, geography, and population, the Grand Duchy of Luxembourg has long based its foreign policy on active participation in multilateral cooperation and integration. It should come as no surprise then, that in 1945, Luxembourg became a founding member of the UN.

Peace and security, development, and human rights are the three fundamental pillars of the UN. For sixty-five years, Luxembourg has helped lead the way in meeting these critical objectives.

Luxembourg proves its commitment to the UN, its goals, and principles not only by honoring its financial obligations under the Charter, but also by making regular voluntary contributions to numerous activities of the UN and its funds and programmes. "We are building bridges and advancing critical issues. That is a major role for us at the UN," said Ambassador Sylvie Lucas, permanent representative. "We see ourselves as honest brokers and true mediators with the responsibility and the capability to bring key issues to the forefront."

Jean Asselborn, Luxembourg minister of foreign affairs and immigration (2004–) and Ban Ki-moon, secretary-general of the UN (2007–).

Luxembourg pursues an active policy of development cooperation, currently allocating more than one percent of its gross national income (GNI) for official development assistance (ODA), surpassing the benchmark established by the United Nations, which is an ODA/GNI rate of 0.7 percent.

Most importantly, Luxembourg's dedication to development aid translates into real-world progress. On World Food Day 2009, which addressed the theme of "Achieving Food Security in Times of Crisis," the organization ActionAid published "Who's Really Fighting Hunger?," a report charting the efforts of developing and developed countries in the fight against hunger. In this report, Luxembourg ranked first among developed countries for devoting a significant part of its ODA to the strengthening of food security in emerging countries. This is a single example of the numerous ways in which Luxembourg's strong

Former President Bill Clinton and Ambassador Sylvie Lucas, permanent representative of Luxembourg to the UN (2008–), at an ECOSOC meeting at the UN.

The Gift of Art, the Art of Peace

Irony, tragedy, and hope all play a part in the story of *The Knotted Gun.*

Ironically, it was former Beatle John Lennon who penned the famous lyrics, "Imagine all the people living life in peace," but who died a violent death at the age of forty after being shot four times by a gunman outside his New York City apartment building on December 8, 1980.

The senseless killing led to creation. The legendary musician's tragic death so disturbed his friend, Swedish artist Carl Fredrik Reuterswärd, that it compelled him to produce different variations of a sculpture he called *Non-Violence,* a large replica in bronze of a 45-caliber revolver, the barrel of which is tied into a knot. The gun is cocked, but the knot makes it clear that it will not shoot.

The symbol expresses in a simple and memorable way the universal hope for peace.

The Luxembourg government acquired one of the first three versions of the sculpture and offered it to the United Nations as a gift in 1988. Now known as *The Knotted Gun,* the sculpture stands outside the United Nations in New York, just a few short blocks from 17 Beekman Place.

Jean-Claude Juncker, Luxembourg prime minister (1995–) and Kofi Annan, secretary-general of the UN (1997–2006).

commitment to development aid is helping to bring about positive change in the world.

Contributing to the maintenance of peace and security is another prime goal of the foreign policy of Luxembourg. The United Nations Peacekeeping Operations are a unique and crucial instrument in achieving international peace and security and helping countries torn by conflict create the conditions for lasting peace. Luxembourg has taken, and continues to take, an active part in the UN peacekeeping missions.

Beyond the efforts it makes in development, peacekeeping, and peacebuilding, Luxembourg is a reliable partner in the daily work of the UN and assumes responsibility within the various bodies of the organization under the Charter of the United Nations. Notably, it had the honor to assume the presidency of the 35th General Assembly, and more recently, in

Strengthening Bonds

The signing of a "joint communiqué" formally establishes relations between two countries that wish to strengthen their cooperation on the basis of the principles and values of the Charter of the United Nations and the Vienna Convention on Diplomatic Relations of 1961. Once signed by diplomatic representatives from both countries, a copy of the joint communiqué is provided to the secretary general of the United Nations, who informs all member states of the United Nations of the formal establishment of diplomatic relations.

Ambassador Sylvie Lucas, permanent representative of Luxembourg to the UN and George Talbot, chargé d'affaires ad interim of Guyana to the UN, sign the joint communiqué by which Luxembourg and Guyana established diplomatic relations as of June 17, 2009.

2009, of the Economic and Social Council (ECOSOC).

The main objective of ECOSOC is to promote higher standards of living, full employment, economic and social progress, and development. "The most severe global financial crisis since the Great Depression has wreaked havoc on the world economy, making progress towards these goals more difficult," said Lucas.

Jean Olinger, deputy permanent representative of Luxembourg to the UN (2005–2010).

Luxembourg also assumes an active role in fostering the UN's human rights agenda by striving for an increased respect for political, economic, and social rights as well as promoting important concepts like the responsibility to protect. The grand duchy has been a committed member of the Commission on Human Rights and actively supported the establishment of the new Human Rights Council. "Going forward, we will continue to be proactive and address pressing issues such as the rights to adequate housing, healthcare, and education as well as work toward eradicating racism and violence against women and children," said Jean Olinger, deputy permanent representative.

In fully accepting the responsibilities that stem from its integration in the system of multilateral cooperation, and in the spirit of international solidarity, Luxembourg abides by the statement of former Secretary General Kofi Annan, who, in his report "In Larger Freedom," emphasized that "Humanity will not enjoy security without development, it will not enjoy development without security, and it will not enjoy either without respect for human rights."

ArcelorMittal, a leading Luxembourg-based steel manufacturer, produced the I-beams used in the lower structure of the Freedom Tower at New York's World Trade Center site.

It is also in this spirit that Luxembourg hopes to be able to make a useful contribution to the Security Council of the United Nations in 2013-2014.

Steely Optimism

Nothing tested the mettle of Americans in its recent history more than the events of September 11, 2001. Terrorists struck New York City, and

François Knaff, consul general and executive director of the TIO (2007–).

the World Trade Center fell. The world stood by America that day, including Luxembourg. Five years later, the workers of the world's largest steel company, Luxembourg-based ArcelorMittal, were actively involved in helping the United States recover and rebuild in the wake of this tragedy.

Construction was underway for the new Freedom Tower (now One World Trade Center), a skyscraper to be located within the sixteen-acre World Trade Center site. On July 28, 2006, David W. Dunlap reported in the *New York Times*: "The Freedom Tower began to take shape this week—the shape of large I's—at a steel mill in Differdange, Luxembourg. There, at a plant of the Arcelor company, 805 tons of steel was rolled into enormous column sections that will, by year's end, begin to form the underground structure of the Freedom Tower."

New York Governor George Pataki, along with spokespersons from the Port Authority of New York and New Jersey as well as Silverstein Properties, made the announcement of Arcelor's involvement in the project. In his press statement, the governor called its steel production "another milestone" for construction at the site.

Richard Kielar, a spokesman for the Tischman Construction Corporation, the company responsible for building the skyscraper, told the *New York Times*: "A mill doesn't exist in the U.S. that could produce the jumbo sections required for the lower levels of the Freedom Tower. Arcelor is one of two mills in the world that can."

North American corporate executives attend a presentation about prosperous sectors of Luxembourg's economy.

ArcelorMittal—formed when Arcelor merged with its rival, Mittal Steel, in 2006 and now present in more than sixty countries—had delivered steel for several notable New York City buildings before, including 7 World Trade Center, the Hearst Tower, the Bank of America Tower at 1 Bryant Park, and the new New York Times Building.

Indeed, the Grand Duchy of Luxembourg has long been famous for its high-strength steel production. The country, in fact, grew wealthy during the nineteenth century, when steel from national iron ore mines fuelled the industry. At its peak, Luxembourg was the seventh-largest steel producer in the world. Today, Luxembourg's steel industry continues to thrive.

Achievements in the steel and other industries have led Luxembourg to remarkable economic development. During the second half of the twentieth century, it achieved one of the strongest

The Luxembourg American Business Award: Testimony to a Friendship

The Luxembourg American Business Award was established in 1999. Presented bi-annually, it recognizes a North American company for its unique and lasting contribution to trade and business with Luxembourg, as well as for its commitment to strengthening the longstanding relationship between the two nations.

Planned and organized at 17 Beekman Place as a collaborative effort between the Luxembourg American Chamber of Commerce and the Trade and Investment Office, the award acknowledges Luxembourg's openness to foreign trade and investment as well as the success achieved by a North American company as a result of that policy

Corporate recipients have included Avery Dennison, Delphi, DuPont, Goodyear, Guardian, and Husky.

H.R.H. Crown Prince Guillaume of Luxembourg bestows the award on the corporate CEO representing his or her company during a black tie event attended by over three-hundred guests from the business community and the Luxembourg government.

H.R.H. Crown Prince Guillaume of Luxembourg, honorary chairman of the Luxembourg Board of Economic Development (2000–) and Jeannot Krecké, Luxembourg minister of the economy and foreign trade (2004–).

Tradition dictates that the Luxembourg American Business Award trophy is novel each time—specially designed by an artist from Luxembourg. It is as unique as the friendship it commemorates.

performances in Europe: sustained economic growth, outstanding price stability, a very low rate of unemployment, and constant growth in employment.

The Right Setting for Serious Business

Although the steel industry provided the foundation for the grand duchy's robust economy, over the years, the Luxembourg government instituted a plan of diversification, economic development, and foreign business attraction to the country. At 17 Beekman Place, both the TIO and LACC have contributed to the advancement of business relationships between American companies and Luxembourg.

The picturesque Banque et Caisse d'Epargne de l'Etat (BCEE) is just one of Luxembourg's many reputable financial institutions.

The purpose of the TIO is to attract U.S. companies to conduct business in Luxembourg—often through innovative solutions and strategic alliances—as well as to support Luxembourg companies in partnering with American companies. The executive director and his team identify North American corporations and motivate their interest in conducting business in Luxembourg. They visit them at their headquarters and also host face-to-face meetings at 17 Beekman Place, where opportunities are developed and pursuant meetings with appropriate Luxembourg authorities are planned and scheduled.

The Luxembourg House is an ideal setting for forging these partnerships, where North American firms meet with government members and learn about investment opportunities in the grand duchy. "As a representative of the TIO, my goal is to educate American companies about the dynamic Luxembourg economy as well as to learn about the specific needs and interests of those companies," said François Knaff, executive director of the TIO. "Once we have

The Luxembourg Financial Center: A Platform for Growth and Innovation

The Luxembourg Financial Center is one of the world's preeminent hosts of sophisticated banking and finance. Comprising close to 150 world-class financial institutions, it is the second-largest global investment fund center after the United States, the leading private banking center in the Eurozone, and the premier captive insurance market in the European Union.

The financial center's success is founded on the social and political stability of Luxembourg and on a modern, evolving legal and regulatory framework resulting from an ongoing collaboration among the government, the legislator, and the private sector. The center has developed innovative regulatory frameworks for alternative investment funds, venture capital investment funds, international pension funds, specialized investment funds, captive reinsurance companies, securitization vehicles, and other financial entities.

Florida-based Arquitectonica designed Banque de Luxembourg, located in Luxembourg City.

This legal framework, combined with Luxembourg's openness to the world, has attracted banks, insurance companies, investment fund promoters, and specialist service providers from around the world.

Claude Kremer, chairman of ALFI (2007–).

The financial center is also home to the Association of the Luxembourg Fund Industry (ALFI), a national organization dedicated to maintaining the high standards of the funds domiciled in Luxembourg, while working with the country's government and within the industry to innovate new products that provide secure, advanced investment opportunities for investors. ALFI conducts a yearly informational "roadshow" in the United States, beginning with a major presentation in New York. 17 Beekman Place is the site of an initial reception featuring ALFI's senior executives and attended by professionals from the financial community.

agreed upon their objectives, I enable the decision-makers to visit Luxembourg and see the country and industry in action. At that point, my role is to connect them with the right authorities in Luxembourg."

According to Knaff, the spirit and approach to doing business in Luxembourg is very similar to that of American business ventures. "Both nations are positive, progressive, and forward-thinking. It is this kind of optimism that fuels our mutual success."

Finance is a thriving sector. Close to 150 banks, subsidiaries, or branches of major banking institutions from twenty-five countries are established in Luxembourg and focus their activities on the international markets. In the grand duchy, these institutions are allowed to operate as "universal banks," spanning the full range of banking activities in the home market and abroad. Luxembourg banks are world-renowned for their sophisticated expertise; the top quality of their multilingual, multinational workforce; and their strict adherence to rules and regulations, overseen by the financial supervisory authority.

An Innovative Environment

At 17 Beekman Place, the executive director of the TIO often poses a question to North American corporate executives: What do eBay, Real Networks, Rovi, Amazon.com, iTunes, and PayPal have in common? These are some of America's most inventive corporations—and they have all chosen to establish their European headquarters in Luxembourg. This should come as no surprise, as like-minded types attract. Both America and Luxembourg take pride in their spirit of innovation.

The grand duchy is an ideal gateway to the major European multimedia, e-commerce, communications, and information technology markets. Due to its international orientation, comprehensive and market-oriented legal system, and state-of-the-art infrastructures, Luxembourg is an appealing environment for content management

Out-of-the-Box Thinking

British science fiction author Arthur C. Clarke did not pen his most famous novel, *2001: A Space Odyssey*, until 1968, but he mused about space and satellites long before then.

In a 1945 article, he explored the idea that geostationary satellites would one day be ideal communications relays.

Years later, in 2004, his dreams were idealized at 17 Beekman Place by native New Yorker photographer Michael Anton in a memorable exhibit depicting the facilities of Luxembourg-based SES, one of the largest companies in the world in the field of satellite communications technology. Seeing beyond function to form, Anton aimed his lens at the company's facilities in Château de Betzdorf, capturing the saucer-like structures against dark, moody skies.

Founded in 1985, SES is the pre-eminent global satellite operator, providing audio-visual entertainment and information as well as business communications and government services. The company's fleet of over forty satellites reach ninety-nine percent of the world's population, transmitting more than thirteen thousand services each day and keeping many of the world's citizens, businesses, and administrations connected.

Oil paint on black & white photo by Michael Anton (above).
SES satellites keep people and businesses connected (below).

and electronic data processing activities in Europe.

In fact, it is home to some of the continent's leading companies in the field, including SES, the world's pre-eminent satellite operator; RTL Group, Europe's largest broadcaster; and Skype, the pioneering Internet communications company. This impressive roster is one reason why North American companies are drawn to Luxembourg.

Today, a plethora of favorite pastimes involve technology,

including downloading and listening to music, playing video games, shopping online, and communicating with friends through social networking. In this digital age, North American companies need a reliable partner to provide the connectivity to deliver real-time, advanced voice and data communications to customers across Europe. That progressive partner is Luxembourg.

Logistics is yet another area of strength. Imagine a U.S. company that

FLYING COLORS!

Cargolux, Luxembourg's flagship freight carrier, is the largest all-cargo airline in Europe, and one of the top ten worldwide. Flying Boeing 747s around the globe, Cargolux is the carrier of choice for many of the world's major corporations, as well as companies shipping unique goods that require special handling, including artwork en route to 17 Beekman Place.

The company is integrated into the Cargocenter at Luxembourg-Findel International Airport, one of the largest freight airports in Europe. The state-of-the art Cargocenter has a capacity of more than one million tons, and it is here that Cargolux provides secure, speedy, and efficient ground handling, enabling jumbo freighter planes to be customs cleared and unloaded at record speeds, as low as ninety minutes.

The Cargocenter provides direct highway access to the European motorway network. Its sophisticated infrastructure and complement of freight forwarders, logistics suppliers, airlines, and trucking companies, allows deliveries to be made to any city on the continent within twenty-four hours of arrival. For these reasons, the Cargocenter and Cargolux itself continue to experience unprecedented growth as they service the needs of clients conducting business around the world.

needs to deliver parts or products to Europe. The central location of the grand duchy makes it an ideal distribution hub to the European market of some five hundred million consumers. An efficient communication and transportation infrastructure strengthens the country's position as a competitive European center for the import and export of goods and services. In fact, Luxembourg's airport is one of the largest freight airports on the continent. Add to that an easier, paperless customs process for importing goods, and the result is less red tape and the ability to do business efficiently.

Georges Faber, consul general and executive director of the BED (2001–2007).

The grand duchy is also a dynamic location for research and development. The country actively participates in the European Union's programs for research and technological advancement. Some of the country's most compelling research activities include international collaborations on behalf of the European Space Agency. The automotive industry is a key high-tech sector for Luxembourg, attracting a high concentration of innovative original equipment manufacturers. It is this kind of technological depth that has drawn many companies from diverse industries to the country. International corporations such as Delphi, Goodyear, and Industrial Electronic Engineers (IEE) have all chosen to locate major research and development centers there.

Intangible assets—creative ideas—play a key role in business growth in today's knowledge-based economy. This might mean original software, new research, even advertising. These creative ideas, often referred to as intellectual property (IP), need to be protected. Intellectual property has become a major driver of economic development as companies migrate their IP portfolios to attractive destinations. In the IP arena, Luxembourg leads the way. The government offers a responsive and supportive environment that stimulates and creates research, rewards innovation and excellence, and promotes intellectual property.

Jean Graff, consul general and executive director of the BED (1995–2001).

Simply stated, in a wide variety of business sectors, Luxembourg has proven to be a genuine innovator.

THE FUTURE OF A NEW SCIENCE

Many thought leaders in the fields of life sciences, biotechnology and medicine agree that the next breakthrough area in healthcare is personalized medicine—the goal of which is to improve prevention, screening, early diagnosis, and treatment of illnesses based on an individual's genetic and biological makeup.

Always an innovator, Luxembourg is helping to lead the way by developing a center of expertise in the area of molecular medicine via a strategic partnership initiative with three world-renowned U.S. research institutions—Translational Genomics Research Institute (TGen), the Institute for Systems Biology (ISB), and the Partnership for Personalized Medicine (PPM). Their projects focus on increasing research in the field of molecular diagnosis, the cornerstone of personalized medicine.

The centerpiece of the overall effort is the creation of a Luxembourg "biobank" in partnership with TGen. The biobank collects and analyzes biological samples and related data to support new oncology research. Additionally, the biobank promotes and facilitates international research projects and aids in translating recent findings into medical practice.

The second part of the project is in collaboration with ISB and aims to establish a center of excellence in systems biology in Luxembourg. Researchers have the opportunity to explore genome sequencing, genetic systems, and molecular fingerprinting. There is a technological component as well—the development and integration of tools used in genomics, proteomics, and bioinformatics.

The third part, carried out with PPM, helps advance breakthrough studies in personalized medicine by pursuing research projects focused on developing molecular diagnostics for specific diseases, such as the selection and validation of biomarkers to more effectively detect and manage lung cancer.

Members of the Trade and Investment Office at 17 Beekman Place have found this ambitious initiative to be an area of keen interest when meeting with North American organizations. The undertaking is testimony to the fact that Luxembourg is fast becoming a genuine health sciences and biotechnology hub, helping the Trade and Investment Office to attract more institutions to Luxembourg, where their progressive research, biotechnology work, and breakthrough discoveries can be rapidly commercialized.

Breakfast and Business

Imagine an executive attending a business event at 17 Beekman Place. What a refreshing change of pace. Rather than a non-descript venue, he or she enters a home—the home of the Luxembourg government in New York. There is a sense of intimacy and warmth. The setting is comfortable, vibrant, and welcoming. At the same time, the place exudes a rich history—a legacy of excellence.

Breakfast seminars are a case in point. The TIO and the LACC host an ongoing series of these as well as business receptions. Attendees include executives from diverse institutions in the city and surrounding areas.

Financial seminar participants (left to right): Rick Lazio, chairman of Financial Services Forum; Luc Frieden, Luxembourg minister of justice, treasury and budget; Jean-Claude Finck, deputy general manager of Luxembourg State Savings Bank; and Thomas Seale, CEO of European Fund Administration S.A. in 2002.

Seminar topics are developed around specific industries that continue to flourish in Luxembourg. Recent topics have included private equity investment in Luxembourg; improving international supply chain issues, tax, valuation, and regulatory aspects of international intellectual properties; telecommunications; and regulatory developments in Luxembourg and Europe, to name a few.

These informative events—held in an uplifting atmosphere—have proven to be of great appeal to New York-area corporations. In addition to corporate speakers and consultants, Luxembourg's ministers of economy and finance have made presentations as well.

With nearly one hundred active members, the LACC is at no loss for members who want to speak about topics of interest to the New York business community. Executives from marquee firms such as Allen & Overy, Arendt & Medernach, Deloitte, Ernst & Young, Houlihan Lokey, HSBC, KPMG, and PricewaterhouseCoopers—all LACC members—have delivered inspiring presentations at the Luxembourg House.

Step Outside

Long before 17 Beekman Place became the diplomatic setting it is today, its inhabitants were drawn to the library. It was James Forrestal's favorite room and the Berlins' middle daughter, Linda Emmet, fondly recalls it as one of the earliest attractions in her new home. On many occasions, Ellin and Irving Berlin enjoyed entertaining guests in the library.

What is the special appeal of this room? Its sense of intimacy, its splendid view...and the lure of what lies beyond its french doors.

Recalling his summers as a child visiting from France, Edward W. Emmet, grandson of Ellin and Irving Berlin, said, "I remember the garden, with the brick floor and a corner where I would sit in a chair and look out at the East River, the Fifty-ninth Street Bridge, and the Pepsi-Cola sign."

Business attendees of a breakfast seminar at the Luxembourg House take a break on the terrace garden.

Just as when the Forrestals and Berlins resided at the house, today, the library opens onto a terrace garden that overlooks the East River. This small slice of paradise remains an enticing oasis for urbanites. It is here that professional networking events are held. Spring on the Terrace and Fall on the Terrace are bi-annual affairs hosted by the TIO. A group of local businesspeople and New York area officials are invited to mix and mingle over cocktails, gaze at the river, and "change your perspective and your view of Luxembourg," according to the executive director of the TIO.

In this relaxed setting, the consul general, members of the LACC, industry consultants, attorneys and others familiar with Luxembourg's economy and industry share information about the many advantages of doing business in the grand duchy.

With its herringbone-patterned brick surface surrounded by evergreens, a plethora of flowers, and even a weeping cherry tree, the terrace garden beckons as it always has, not only for businesspeople, but for community association members as well.

Rue de la Loge is an inviting street in the old town, noted for its charming townhouses, many of which are now fine restaurants, contemporary lounges, and colorful cafes.

A Magical Place to Visit

Seventeen Beekman Place has become a site of interest for numerous neighborhood organizations. With its rich heritage, exquisite architectural features, and lush terrace garden, the charming red brick house is a favorite of local historical, architectural, and garden groups.

Meanwhile, upstairs in their fifth floor offices, members of the National Tourist Office work to promote another magical place to visit: Luxembourg. The primary work of the National Tourist Office is to ensure that the country has a strong presence with U.S. travelers and the tourism community.

"Our goal is to encourage both individuals and groups from the U.S. to visit the grand duchy," said Brigitte Goergen, director of the Luxembourg National Tourist Office. "We know from the positive feedback that we've received from tour operators and visitors that Luxembourg holds great appeal for history buffs, sophisticated travelers, and is an exciting and conducive setting for business conventions."

French architect Christian de Portzamparc designed the breathtaking Philharmonie Concert Hall in Luxembourg City.

Indeed, Luxembourg holds big surprises for American visitors. From modern infrastructure to medieval towns with magnificent castles, from bustling urban centers to unspoiled natural beauty, from countless cultural attractions to boutique and high street shops, there is something for everyone in Luxembourg. Since 1994, the fortifications and old town have been classified as a UNESCO World Heritage site.

Art and music aficionados are never at a loss in the country's capital of Luxembourg City. It is home to many museums, among them

Celebrating Art, Architecture, and Americans

Rural Luxembourg may be the land of castles, but its urban landscape is marked by a modern American influence. Luxembourg City has become an aesthetic home for some of the United States' most prominent artists and architects. From striking steel sculptures to gleaming glass buildings, Americans such as architect Richard Meier, artist Frank Stella, and sculptor Richard Serra have left their signatures on the streets of Luxembourg City.

In 2008, the Luxembourg National Tourist Office partnered with the New York Consulate on the exhibition Famous Americans in Luxembourg: Art & Architecture. The exhibit featured photographs and architectural models of some of contemporary Luxembourg's most breathtaking buildings and environmental sculptures.

Architect I. M. Pei designed Musée d'Art Moderne Grand-Duc Jean (MUDAM).

In a stunning series of photographs, visitors had the opportunity to view the headquarters of Banque de Luxembourg, with its ambitious glass front and impressive exhibition rooms. The Miami, Florida-based architectural firm Arquitectonica designed the building in the 1990s. There were photographs of Serra's steel masterpiece, *Exchange*, created in 1996, which stands as a distinct landmark to the entrance of the city, as well as Stella's fissured steel sculpture, *Sarreguemines*, which is situated on a broad plaza.

Two architectural models were also on display. World-renowned architect I.M. Pei designed Luxembourg's exquisite Musée d'Art Moderne Grand-Duc Jean (MUDAM), artfully blending historical and contemporary elements. The model of the museum, which opened in 2006, was on loan to the National Tourist Office for the special event courtesy of MUDAM.

HypoVereinsbank Luxembourg was built in 1993 based on plans by Meier. Thanks to the generosity of the architect, the model was on loan for the exhibit.

"The event was a way of celebrating great American talents and their role in making Luxembourg City a unique environment in Europe and in the world," said Brigitte Goergen, director of the Luxembourg National Tourist Office.

For a time, 17 Beekman Place momentarily reflected the artistic environment of its cultural home in Europe.

the Musée d'Art Moderne Grand-Duc Jean (MUDAM), which was conceived and designed by renowned architect I.M. Pei and opened in 2006. The museum's collection includes two hundred works of art—from the 1980s to the present—by more than one hundred artists from around the world. However, art lies beyond the city's museum walls as well. Visitors will find an interesting array of it in its public spaces, also—much of which was created by internationally acclaimed architects and artists who have been inspired by the country's natural beauty. Concert halls abound in Luxembourg City, too, and range from traditional venues to innovative performance spaces. The country's most prominent musical ensemble is the Luxembourg Philharmonic Orchestra, based in the city's stunning Philharmonie Concert Hall. Designed by French architect Christian de Portzamparc, the extraordinary building opened in 2005.

In Ettelbruck, a massive statue of U. S. Army General George S. Patton Jr. stands in remembrance. Patton is buried in the Luxembourg American Cemetery and Memorial in Hamm, Luxembourg.

Americans are often drawn to their shared history with the grand duchy. The General Patton Memorial Museum in Ettelbruck contains more than one thousand photographs and documents pertaining to the German invasion of Luxembourg in May 1940, the period of occupation, and the liberation of the country by American troops in September 1944. The National Museum of Military History in Diekirch offers an in-depth education about the Battle of the Bulge in Luxembourg.

Nature lovers are inspired and invigorated by the country's expansive valleys, rugged cliffs, and unique rock formations. A visit to the Ardennes in northern Luxembourg's lush rural setting is ideal for active visitors with its many hiking and biking trails. The Moselle Valley, dating back to the Romans, offers a glorious park, boating, and vineyards. The south of

The Grund is an appealing quarter located in a valley below Luxembourg City on the banks of the Alzette River.

Luxembourg is often referred to as the "land of red rocks," with scenic trails marked with challenging plateaus that run through wooded and grassland areas. Sophisticated mansions built in the art nouveau and art deco styles give this region a touch of elegance.

Léa Linster, Luxembourg's star chef and winner of the 1989 Bocuse d'Or.

Gourmets cannot get enough of the grand duchy. Luxembourg boasts more Michelin-starred restaurants per capita than any other country in the world. Former breweries and colorful townhouses have been transformed into charming settings for a variety of restaurants and bars that welcome a multi-cultural, cosmopolitan population. Moreover, no other country can serve up the likes of Léa Linster. Much more than a star chef, Linster is something of a national treasure. She is the first and only female to have won the prestigious Bocuse d'Or world cuisine contest. Founded in 1987 by chef Paul Bocuse, and held every two years in Lyon, France, the Bocuse d'Or is considered the world's most rigorous international culinary competition.

Indeed, the grand duchy is rich in historical, cultural, culinary, and natural resources. The National Tourist Office works closely with American tour operators and travel agents, promoting Luxembourg's unique offerings. Organizing trips specifically for tour operators and travel agents is essential so that they may experience the grand duchy first-hand. These site inspections typically include guided tours to Luxembourg City, Clervaux, Vianden, Echternach, and the Moselle. Agents have a chance to sample the cuisine, take in the scenery and the sites, and enjoy the cultural and historical offerings of the country.

Luxembourg has something for everyone—nightlife, cultural and culinary delights, a bucolic countryside and family fun.

Building relationships with the media is one of the most important aspects of the work of the National Tourist Office. Its director works diligently to secure press coverage about Luxembourg with national travel-related media. "When we speak with

Visitors enjoy exploring Luxembourg's many biking trails.

journalists, we emphasize the quality and diversity that Luxembourg offers to travelers," said Goergen. "In Luxembourg City, visitors will find top museums and beautiful architecture, and yet the entire country is such a manageable place to visit. It is easy to get around and within twenty minutes, you can go from the city to the countryside. It is an ideal place for families."

Over the years, the group has generated articles about the grand duchy's appeal as an attractive destination in the *New York Times*, the *Boston Globe*, the *Chicago Tribune*, the *Los Angeles Times*, and *Travel+Leisure*, to name a few. In recent years, gaining exposure in online media has been a growing and important trend in reaching travelers. The National Tourist Office has built a strong rapport with editors of travel Web sites, bloggers, and young journalists who find innovative avenues for spreading the message about Luxembourg's many delights—from castles to culture to bucolic wine country.

Brigitte Goergen, director of the Luxembourg National Tourist Office (2003–).

"Hardly any other European capital city serves up such an impressive array of contrasts as Luxembourg's," said Goergen. "In the grand duchy, you'll find a one-thousand-year-old city, that is also a prosperous and innovative metropolis."

A Spirit of Community

Another central purpose of the Luxembourg House is to serve as a gathering place for the country's citizens living in and around the area. At 17 Beekman Place, Luxembourgish traditions are embraced, and a spirit of community flourishes.

Every Luxembourger—here and abroad—pays homage to the grand duchy on its National Day. Celebrated on June 23, the day honors the birthday of the sovereign. Each year on that day, the

EDWARD STEICHEN: THE GREAT CONNECTOR

Although American, the ingenious photographer, educator, and innovator Edward Steichen left his greatest legacy in Luxembourg, the country of his birth.

Born in Bivange in 1879, Steichen considered The Family of Man, his exhibition depicting the oneness of mankind throughout the world, to be the most important work of his life. For the exhibition, Steichen selected over five hundred pictures by photographers from sixty-eight countries and grouped them around universal themes such as love, birth, death, and hope. The Family of Man debuted in 1955 at New York City's Museum of Modern Art and subsequently toured in thirty-seven countries. Steichen's wish was that The Family of Man would ultimately reside in the country of his birth, so the U.S. government offered the collection to the grand duchy, where it is permanently housed at the Castle of Clervaux. In 2003, The Family of Man was added to UNESCO's Memory of the World Register.

Edward Steichen's world-renowned photo collection, The Family of Man, on display at the Castle of Clervaux, is listed on UNESCO's Memory of the World Register for its outstanding universal value.

One of Luxembourg's most prestigious art awards was inspired by the memory of Steichen. Established in 2005, the primary aim of the Edward Steichen Award is to create an opportunity for young European artists to work in New York City, one of the world's great artistic centers. Its secondary aim is to foster cross-cultural links between the art and cultural communities of Luxembourg and New York. Presented every two years in Luxembourg, recipients have included Su-Mei Tsé (2006), Etienne Boulanger (2008), and Bertille Bak (2010).

Irving Berlin with first daughter Mary Ellin Barrett, and Ellin Berlin holding newborn second daughter Linda Emmet. The photograph was taken by Edward Steichen in 1932.

Luxembourg House hosts a commemorative party. Traditional Luxembourgish dishes are served, guests enjoy a glass of Crémant or a Luxembourg Riesling, and invitees join in singing "Ons Heemecht" ("Our Homeland"), the grand duchy's national anthem.

Luxembourg National Day celebration.

The holiday season brings with it several traditions including an annual Christmas party as well as a St. Nicholas event designed specifically for the youngest members of the Luxembourg community in and around the city. Moreover, a Christmas Eve tradition, begun by one of Irving Berlin's musical neighbors in the early 1980s, continues well into the twenty-first century, thanks to admiring fans of Berlin's songs and support from the Luxembourg government.

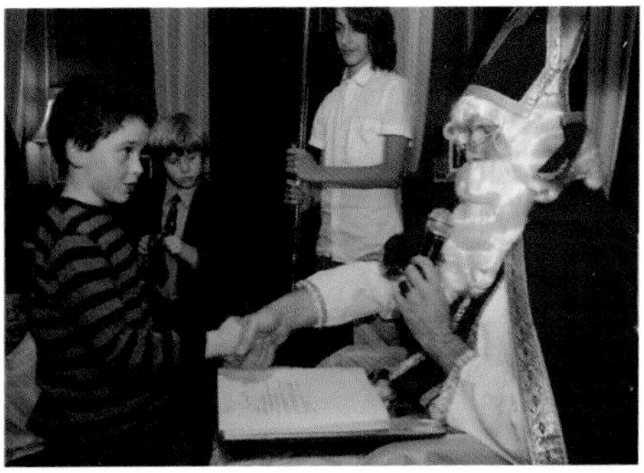

An annual St. Nicholas event for children is a tradition.

It was Christmas Eve 1983 when cabaret singer, songwriter, and longtime Beekman Place neighbor John Wallowitch first led a small group of talented friends and colleagues to the corner of Fiftieth Street and Beekman Place. There, in front of Berlin's home, they serenaded the famous composer with renditions of two of his most popular tunes, "White Christmas" and "Always."

The musical group continued the holiday songfest until the songwriter died in late 1989. Out of respect, they did not sing in front of the house that Christmas. But a year later, Wallowitch gathered a group of singers to resume the seasonal salute to the beloved composer. When the Grand Duchy of Luxembourg bought the house, the Christmas Eve tradition was given a boost. Each year, the Luxembourg House awaits the arrival of the carolers (since Wallowitch's death in 2007, it has been organized by a musical colleague, Bobb Goldsteinn), enjoys their singing, and then invites them into the house for holiday refreshments.

The late John Wallowitch, cabaret singer, songwriter, and former neighbor of Irving Berlin, started an annual Christmas salute to Berlin at the house.

While celebrating traditions is important, serving the

community is an even higher priority at 17 Beekman Place. The Consulate manages a wide variety of administrative duties including the renewal of passports for Luxembourg citizens as well as issuing visas for international travelers seeking to visit the grand duchy. "Our goal is to expedite the process so that travelers have the opportunity to explore Luxembourg's business and cultural attractions," said Saba Amroun-Febres, executive assistant to the consul general.

A Cultural Venue

"While a strong economy is the backbone of a country, its artists represent the soul of a nation," said Laurence Pierron, executive assistant to the executive director of the TIO. "The grand duchy recognizes the invaluable contributions of its indigenous artists, and that spirit extends to 17 Beekman Place."

The Luxembourg House hosts an eclectic mix of cultural events including concerts, art and photography exhibitions, film screenings, and book signings. Their primary purpose is to showcase the talents of native Luxembourg artists and provide them with a platform for exposure in New York. For Luxembourgers residing in the area, these events serve as a bridge, linking them to their homeland and reinforcing their sense of pride in their country. For the American audience also in attendance, the goal is to generate interest in Luxembourg by celebrating its rich and unique culture.

The former living room on the second floor often awaits an audience. Music performances—from classical recitals to jazz ensembles—take place here.

Irving Berlin's Steinway grand piano made a striking statement on the second floor for more than forty years. Today, the second floor continues to resonate with music as a performance space for Luxembourg musicians inclined to make their own creative statements. Over the years, the Luxembourg House has played host to numerous musical events—covering virtually every genre—and has showcased over one hundred musicians.

Running Away, Coming Back Home

Envision late October in New York City. There is an invigorating nip in the air. The leaves have just begun to fall in Central Park and nature's colors are everywhere. Several thousand runners from around the world have gathered for the annual New York City Marathon. A contingency from Luxembourg—some 40 strong—led for the past ten years by Roland Hoferlin, a former New York City marathon runner, is among them. Dawn has barely broken and they are off—and running.

The next day, they come back home—to 17 Beekman Place.

Since 1996, the Consulate General has hosted a special luncheon reception to honor Luxembourg citizens who have competed in the marathon. After rigorous preparation and a tough race, it is time to indulge. A buffet is served, along with wines from the grand duchy. The event is festive, fun, and unforgettable.

The Consulate General and the Luxembourg National Tourist Office turned the media spotlight on the grand duchy's marathoners when they booked a guest appearance for the entire group on the *CBS Early Show* with Harry Smith, making the group celebrities for a day. At 17 Beekman Place, the marathoners—and all Luxembourg citizens who visit—are VIPs everyday.

Composer and pianist Francesco Tristano Schlimé was still a student at the Juilliard School when he first performed a classical recital at the Luxembourg House in 1997. However, this would hardly be the last time Schlimé would fill its elegant rooms with his sounds of music. He returned for three additional appearances, and his evolution as an artist was evident. Although classically trained, Schlimé had embraced jazz by 2003. During an evening called Jazz & Art at the Luxembourg House, Schlimé led a lively quartet including two fellow Luxembourgers, percussionist Jérôme Goldschmidt and drummer, composer, and bandleader Paul Wiltgen, a Manhattan School of Music graduate, along with American bassist William Perry Wortman.

Violinist Johnny Gandelsman and pianist Francesco Tristano Schlimé.

Jazz, a distinctly American art form, is particularly popular. Numerous musicians from Luxembourg have embraced it, bringing their own experiences and voices to the genre. Often, jazz artists from Luxembourg and America play together at the Luxembourg House. This kind of creative collaboration—and mutual appreciation of one another's cultures—is in keeping with the special connection and friendship Luxembourg and America have long shared.

Ernie Hammes.

Michel Reis, a pianist from Luxembourg, and second prize winner at the 2006 Montreux Jazz Solo Piano Competition, has performed with his jazz trio, which featured two Americans, bassist and composer Michael Oien and Eric Doob on drums and percussion.

Michel Reis.

The Consulate also welcomed Ernie Hammes. A classical soloist as well as a jazz trumpet player, Hammes toured extensively with the internationally famous big band leader Maynard Ferguson from 2001 to 2004. However, when Hammes took center stage it was as jazz leader. The Ernie Hammes Group—featuring players from France and Germany on saxophone, piano, bass and drums—delivered a stellar performance. Hammes later returned to the Luxembourg House to appear along with

Jérôme Goldschmidt's Latin Jazz Ensemble.

Americans Jay Anderson, bassist, and Jay Rosen, drummer, in a multi-media performance, *Jazz and Film Noir*: "La Femme Fatale," which was conceived and created by Luxembourg resident, writer, and filmmaker Ana Isabel Ordonez.

It was all mambo beats the night Jérôme Goldschmidt's Latin Jazz Ensemble performed. An audience of more than one hundred swayed to the sounds of salsa and merengue as the Luxembourgish percussionist—celebrating his ten-year career in New York, including performances with the Tito Puente Orchestra—led a lively and talented group of musicians from the United States, Germany, and Puerto Rico.

Recognizing the depth and diversity of Luxembourg's rich musical heritage, the Consulate's cultural division has featured classical concerts, contemporary music, and traditional folk music as well.

Jean Muller, a classical pianist who has performed on many large stages around the world, including the Philharmonie Luxembourg, made his U.S. debut in a recital at the Luxembourg House. John Gerlach, director of the Tri-Institutional Noon Recitals, was in attendance and commissioned Muller to perform in his hall at New York's Rockefeller University.

On the other end of the musical spectrum, Dream Catcher rocked the Luxembourg House. The European Music Organization scheduled a New York tour for the well-known Luxembourgish pop-rock band, and the Consulate was an important stop along the way.

Jean Muller made his U.S. debut with a solo classical recital at the Luxembourg House.

Artful Walls

The walls of the house have always been adorned with art, from the Forrestals' paintings by twentieth-century artists to the Boldini portrait

To Dream, To Dance

Aspiring dancers the world over dream of the chance to set foot on a New York City stage. That is precisely what happened in 2007 for fifty-two young dancers, aged thirteen to eighteen, all students of the Li Marteling Dance Studio in Luxembourg.

The Consulate General arranged for the troupe to perform its annual jazz and hip-hop show at the Turtle Bay Music School, which Josephine Forrestal had supported some seventy-five years earlier. The stage was set, invitations were mailed, and the young dancers, appreciative of this rare opportunity, were on their toes! *Just Dancing 2007* drew an enthusiastic audience of 130.

Following the performance, a festive celebration was held at 17 Beekman Place. Once again, the house was teeming with young people as it had when the Berlins held parties for their daughters and friends there. While the adults enjoyed cocktails on the second floor, the library was the domain of the dancers. Colorful photographs of dancers lined the walls. A lavish meal was served. Spilling out onto the terrace garden under the stars, excitedly conversing, many a young dancer's dream came true that delightful evening.

of Ellin Berlin's mother that found its place of honor on the west wall of the former living room. A tradition of showcasing fine art continues today at the Luxembourg House.

The Consulate sponsors an array of exhibitions featuring the paintings, photography, sculpture, and other artistic creations of Luxembourgish artists. American and other international artists who have chosen Luxembourg as a thematic subject have also had their works on display. Openings are held in much the same manner as those of a traditional art gallery.

An enthusiastic audience comprised of New Yorkers and Luxembourgers responds to an evening's performance.

Ranked among Luxembourg's most recognized contemporary artists, Robert Brandy's paintings are found in many art museums and collections around the world, including at Carnegie Hall in New York. Brandy's work on canvas was the first exhibition held at the house. Due to its tremendous success, he made a second appearance with Jazz and Art at the Luxembourg House, combining his colorful paintings with the sounds of jazz performed by local Luxembourg musicians.

At the Luxembourg House, art exhibitions take place on the second floor, including in the former dining room.

Elisabeth Calmes, a well-known painter throughout Europe, showcased her work at a gallery in Texas before arriving at 17 Beekman Place. The exhibition Luxembourg-Paris-New York displayed paintings of her native country and city of residence as well as some of her temporary New York residence. From a studio in DUMBO (a Brooklyn

Left to right: Brigitte Goergen, director of the Luxembourg National Tourist Office (2003–); Fernand Lamesch, chairman of the LACC (2006–); Roseline Koener, painter.

neighborhood), Calmes captured the spirit of her new city and returned to the Luxembourg House with her new collection, While Meandering Through New York, an allegory of the city, its boroughs, and its landmarks, but also its neighborhood townhouses. The walls reverberated with vibrant colors and energy executed on canvas and cardboard. Only the sound of New York City traffic was missing!

A Luxembourg native and a New York resident, Roseline Koener has exhibited her paintings on two occasions. Textures of Fire showcased her simple interplay of colors and everyday materials, influenced by the rich culture and lively pulse of Africa. Rather than traditional canvases, Koener used textured materials such as Nepalese paper as her canvases, layering them with fabric and paint. Following this show, Textures of Fire was exhibited at New York's Walter Wickiser Gallery.

Reflection (alabaster, marble) by Vicky Hinger.

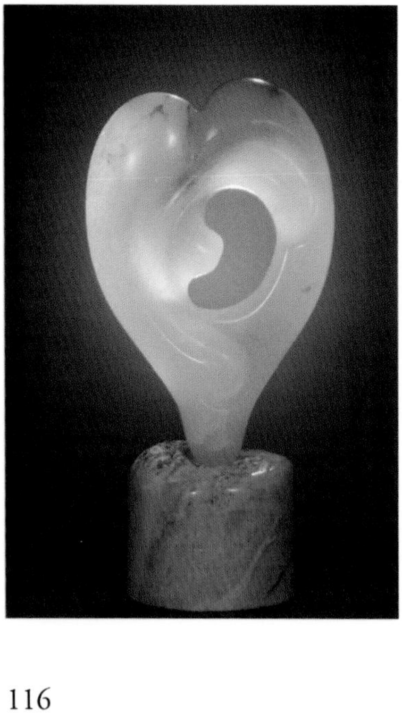

Luxembourg-born and U.S. resident, sculptor Vicky Hinger, presented Stonelegance, an exhibition inspired by her encounters with the Aboriginal people and African tribes during her traveling years. Hinger's creations in limestone, alabaster, and marble employ tastefully associated colors and shades, combining tarnished and shiny textures in unique forms and shapes, at times defying gravity.

The Consulate actively seeks out innovative exhibitions such as Elegance and Nature. This show featured the creations of two Luxembourg-born artists, a painter and a jewelry designer who shared a common theme—both found their inspiration in nature. Through simple, fine brushstrokes of black paint on stark white canvases, Véronique Rischard's series was a tribute to trees. Her executions ranged from miniatures to large-scale paintings to triptychs. Patrice Parisotto transformed natural materials including stones, pearls, and coral into artful and original jewelry.

In 2008, a tribute to ten glorious women from Luxembourg was the focus of a special event. Native writer Katja Rausch partnered with painter and illustrator Iva Mrazkova on the book *Portraits de Femmes Célèbres Luxembourgeoises.* The event included an exhibition of Mrazkova's original portraits of famous Luxembourgish women featured in its pages, including illustrations of Louise Welter, Luxembourg's first female doctor and a pioneer in implementing medical assistance in the country's school system. The author, who had done extensive research and interviewed family members of the ten heroines, autographed books for a receptive audience.

The Consulate presents ongoing exhibitions of works by contemporary Luxembourg artists such as Véronique Rischard.

Today, the Luxembourg House carries on a tradition of showcasing contemporary artists from the grand duchy who are living proof of a nation filled with rich messages and creative minds.

The Screening Room

One of Irving Berlin's pastimes while residing on Beekman Place was watching movies with friends. Though the projection booth he installed in the back of the library is long gone, the tradition of sharing films continues today on the house's second floor. The Consulate sponsors numerous screenings including documentaries, animated movies, and avant-garde art films. On such occasions, the former living room—now outfitted with portable high-tech projection equipment—is transformed into an intimate, comfortable, screening room.

It was a big personality that first showed up on the room's big screen. Luxembourgish historian Paul Lesch wrote a book, *Playing Her Part: Perle Mesta in Luxembourg,* about the flamboyant American diplo-

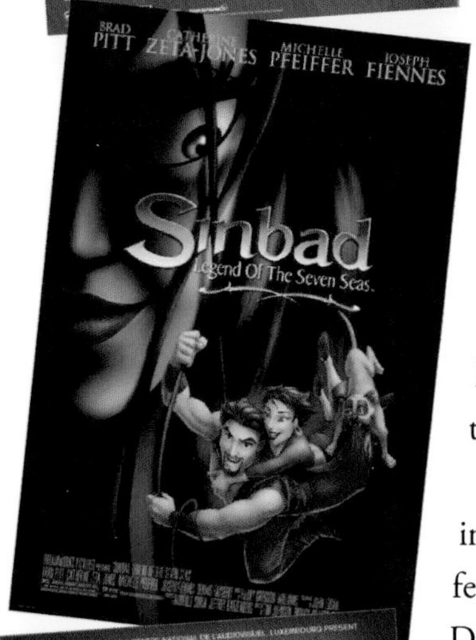

mat. Later, he directed and produced a documentary film, *Call Her Madam* (Samsa Film, 1997), based on his book. In 2002, the documentary was presented in conjunction with a book signing. More than fifty years since Irving Berlin began work on his musical about "the hostess with the mostess," his former home was once again filled with the spirit of Perle Mesta.

Luxembourgish communities in the United States were the subject of the 2007 documentary *Luxembourg, USA* by writer and director Christophe Wagner and producer Willy Perelsztejn. Between 1830 and 1900, approximately seventy thousand Luxembourgers emigrated to the United States to begin a new life. The film explores the history and the reasons for this mass emigration, primarily to America's rural heartland. For many Americans in attendance, the documentary was a history lesson about Luxembourgers' unique cultural contributions to America's Midwest.

Perhaps one of the most compelling film screenings was *Léif Lëtzebuerger-Charlotte: A Royal at War*. The feature-length documentary tells the true story of Grand Duchess Charlotte of Luxembourg and her exile during the grand duchy's brutal occupation by Hitler's Third Reich. Charlotte inspired a nation through her regular BBC radio broadcasts, reaching her people in their darkest hour and keeping hope alive. The film explores Charlotte's friendship with President Franklin D. Roosevelt and her fearless fight for Luxembourg's liberation.

The project was conceived by Candice Allen-Olson. Written and directed by Ray Tostevin and produced by Allen-Olson and Lynn Rothwell of GRACE Productions, the documentary combines eyewitness testimony with dramatic reconstruction and unique, previously unseen, color archival footage.

First released in Luxembourg in 2008, and later that same year in London, *Léif Lëtzebuerger-Charlotte: A Royal at War* made its U.S. debut at the Luxembourg House in March 2009. Special guests at the event included Curtis Roosevelt, grandson of the late president, who autographed his book *Too Close to the Sun*, as well as Battle of the Bulge veteran John Colligan. Both men recount their wartime experiences in the film.

Guests mingle on the second floor landing during a reception following a cultural event.

The riveting documentary brought tears to the eyes of an audience comprised of both Luxembourgers and Americans. As the final image faded and the credits rolled, it was a cathartic and communal moment. *Léif Lëtzebuerger-Charlotte: A Royal at War* is not only a powerful portrait of one woman's remarkable allegiance to her people, but also of America's and Luxembourg's allegiance to one another.

Honoring a Legend

Among the multitude of cultural events produced, none befit the house and its heritage better than those that honor the legacy of Irving Berlin. The staff members of the house take great pride in presenting events that continue to shine a spotlight on the legendary American songwriter. Interestingly, not all of these activities are musical performances.

From left: Curtis Roosevelt, grandson of FDR; Candice Allen-Olson and Lynn Rothwell, producers of *Léif Lëtzebuerger-Charlotte: A Royal at War*, and François Knaff, consul general (2007 –).

Writers have long been inspired by the story of Irving Berlin. After David Leopold's book *Irving Berlin's Show Business* was published in 2005, the

David Leopold, author of a 2005 book about the American songwriter, held a book signing event at the Luxembourg House.

Rodgers & Hammerstein Organization, which represents the Irving Berlin Music Company, contacted the Consulate and requested use of the house for a book signing, which the songwriter's grandson, Edward W. Emmet, attended.

Visual artists have drawn their inspiration from Irving Berlin as well. Luxembourger Diane Jodes and American Robert Hall celebrated him in the exhibition Revisiting Irving Berlin. Jodes, who works in mixed media, contributed a number of pieces including *The Music Box*, a shadow-box work featuring a miniature piano keyboard and a collage of sheet music, memorabilia, and photographs—artfully framed by a classic red velvet theater curtain. The show also featured a series of drawings by Hall that reflected his interpretation of Berlin's life and times.

"Irving Berlin was a remarkable man, and late nineteenth to early twentieth century America is a fascinating era," said Robert Hall. "Reading, viewing images and listening to music from this period, in particular that of Irving Berlin, has awakened my identity as an American, understanding better where we have come from."

Perhaps nothing keeps the Berlin legacy alive more than the tradition of musical performances known as Irving Berlin Salons at the Luxembourg House. In this ongoing series, featuring amateurs and professionals from the diverse worlds of cabaret, opera, and Broadway, the composer's familiar songs continue to echo throughout the townhouse.

"Using the house as a place for cultural events is a wonderful outcome," said Emmet. "It provides an opportunity to promote Luxembourgish artists in New York City, as well as remind their audience of the memory and contributions of my grandfather."

Edward W. Emmet, grandson of Ellin and Irving Berlin, has frequently attended events at the house.

One of the most illustrious salons—Songs from *Call Me Madam*—took place in May 2007. It was produced by special arrangement with the Rodgers & Hammerstein Organization. For two consecutive evenings, four talented opera students from New York's Mannes College sang the show's tunes, as Berlin's legendary story about Perle Mesta was narrated by Ted Chapin, president and executive director of the Rodgers & Hammerstein Organization.

Fifty-nine years after *Call Me Madam* opened on Broadway, Broadway debuted at 17 Beekman Place. In the words of a favorite Berlin tune, "...good luck came a-knocking at my door."

Opera students after their performance of Songs from *Call Me Madam* with Georges Faber, consul general (2001–2007) (center).

"White Christmas" at the Luxembourg House took place during the 2009 holiday season and featured Broadway singers Glory Crampton and Kevin Earley accompanied by Ross Patterson on piano. The trio performed Berlin's classic "White Christmas" along with other tunes from the songwriter's repertoire. Interestingly, Crampton has her own special link to Berlin. Her great grandfather, composer A. Baldwin Sloane, worked alongside him as a founding member of the American Society of Composers, Authors and Publishers (ASCAP).

During an enchanting evening of music and celebration, the songs of Irving Berlin rang through the halls of his former home. Thanks to Luxembourg's tradition of supporting the arts, his melodies and memories live on.

• • •

Broadway performers Kevin Earley and Glory Crampton take center stage at the Luxembourg House.

Seventeen Beekman Place, a graceful Neo-Georgian townhouse realized at a highly improbable time, remains one of New York's architectural treasures. But it is the accomplishments of its inhabitants—innovators who made exceptional imprints on American finance, government, and the arts—that make its legacy all the more remarkable.

Imagined by a Wall Street banker whose dedication to success propelled him to the highest levels of patriotic service, then beloved by a songwriter who literally changed the lexicon of his country's music, 17 Beekman Place continues to imbue an exceptionally inventive spirit. Today, multiple entities of the Luxembourg government engage in a host of international diplomatic, economic, consular, and cultural initiatives in the house, continually forging progressive partnerships with the United States and the world. Standing as a witness to history in a quiet cul-de-sac overlooking the East River, this distinguished residence will be forever recognized for the invaluable contributions of those who have lived, and now work, within its storied walls.

View of 17 Beekman Place from the north with the East River beyond.

1999: The Goodyear Tire & Rubber Company. Presented to Samir G. Gibara, chairman of the board, CEO, and president, by H.R.H. Crown Prince Henri of Luxembourg. The Plaza Hotel, New York. Award designer: Jeannot Bewing.

2002: Dupont Corporation. Presented to Charles O. Holliday Jr., chairman and CEO, by H.R.H. Crown Prince Guillaume of Luxembourg. Cipriani 42nd Street, New York. Award designer: Liliane Heidelberger.

A Gallery of Photograph

2004: Guardian Industries Corporation. Presented to William M. Davidson, president and CEO, by H.R.H. Crown Prince Guillaume of Luxembourg. Center: Fernand Lamesch, president, LACC. The Rainbow Room, New York. Award designer: Pascale Seil.

2006: Avery Dennison Corporation. Presented to Dean A. Scarborough, pres dent and CEO, by H.R.H. Crown Prince Guillaume of Luxembourg. Mandarin Oriental, New York. Award designer: Vicky Hinger. Left to right: Georges Fabe consul general of Luxembourg in New York; Michel Franck, president, LACC Jeannot Krecké, minister of the economy and foreign trade; Dean A. Scarborough; Vicki Hart, manager, internal and electronic communications, Aver Dennison; H.R.H. Crown Prince Guillaume of Luxembourg; Vicky Hinger; Fernand Lamesch, chairman, LACC; Toni Dudsak, executive director, LACC.

2008 Delphi Corporation. Presented to Rodney O'Neal, CEO and president, by H.R.H. Crown Prince Guillaume of Luxembourg. Gotham Hall, New York. Award designer: Patrick Ripp. Left to right: Michel Franck, president, LACC; Fernand Lamesch, chairman, LACC; Jeannot Krecké, minister of the economy and foreign trade; H.R.H. Crown Prince Guillaume of Luxembourg; Steven A. Kiefer, vice president, Delphi Corporation; Toni Dudsak, executive director, LACC; Rodney O'Neal; François Knaff, consul general of Luxembourg in New York.

lew York City Mayor Michael R. Bloomberg (center) with (left to right): eannot Krecké, minister of the economy and foreign trade; H.R.H. Crown Prince Guillaume of Luxembourg; Mrs. William (Karen) Davidson; ean Asselborn, minister of foreign ffairs and immigration; William M. avidson, president and CEO, Guardian ndustries (award recipient); Georges aber, consul general; 2004.

1990 – Present

eft to right: Marshall D. Andrews, global business line executive, elphi; Fernand Lamesch, chairman, LACC; Steven A. Kiefer, vice resident, Delphi; Deborah Lee Ayers, regional director, Delphi; oni Dudsak, executive director, LACC; Georges Schmit, Ministry f the Economy and Foreign Trade; Carine Knaff-Feipel; François naff, consul general; 2008.

Joseph Weyland, ambassador of Luxembourg to the U.S., and Dr. Mary Trefry, associate professor and chair of the Management Department, Sacred Heart University, 2006.

Brenda Russell, manager of global accounts/North America, Cargolux Airlines International, 2006.

Jean-Paul Senninger, ambassador of Luxembourg to the U.S., 2008.

atrick Nickels, Ministry of the Economy, nd James D. Moore, group vice-president, managing director/Europe, Guardian ndustries; 2004.

Ann L. Wagner, U.S. ambassador to Luxembourg (2005-2009), and Georges Schmit, Ministry of the Economy and Foreign Trade; 2008.

Raymond J. Learsy, LACC, 2004.

Luxembourg Trade and Investment Office and LACC Economic Missions and Seminars

H.R.H. Crown Prince Henri of Luxembourg and Robert Goebbels, minister of the economy, on a U.S. economic mission; 1997.

Economic mission participants (left to right): Patrick Nickels, Ministry of the Economy; Georges Faber, consul general; Gaston Reinesch, Ministry of Finance; Henri Grethen, minister of the economy; Georges Schmit, Ministry of the Economy; and Robert Biwer, consul general of Luxembourg in San Francisco; 2003.

Welcome reception for Claude Wiseler, minister for sustainable development and infrastructure. Left to right: Jerry Seeman, Luxcore; Claude Wiseler; Georges Friden, Ministry of Foreign Affairs and Immigration; François Knaff, consul general; Michel Franck, president, LACC; Lawrence J. Blascovich, HSBC (New York); 2009.

LACC breakfast seminar attendees (left to right): Lydie Polfer, minister of foreign affairs and foreign trade; Fernand Lamesch, president of LACC; and Arlette Conzemius, ambassador of Luxembourg to the U.S.; 1999.

Arendt & Medernach private equity seminar participants (left to right): Francis Kass, Constance Jacobs, Cynthia Kalathas, Carine Feipel, Guy Harles, and Sébastien Binard, 2008.

Luxembourg, the Gateway Between U.S. and China tax seminar leader Dirk Dewitte, Deloitte S.A. (Luxembourg), 2008.

Intellectual Property seminar speaker Jurjan Wouda Kuipers, Ernst & Young (New York), 2009.

Craig Dudsak, Citibank, and Patricia Catalano-Rasmussen, LACC, 2009.

Allen & Overy investment funds seminar leaders (left to right): Gabriel Bleser, Patrick Goebel, Marc Feider, and Patrick Mischo, 2009.

Tax partner Louis Thomas, KPMG (Luxembourg), 2008.

Luxembourg Trade and Investment Office and LACC Economic Missions and Seminars

Pierre Gramegna, Luxembourg Chamber of Commerce, 2008.

Luxembourg Investment Fund presentation panelists (left to right): Manuel Mouget, Alter Domus (Luxembourg); Adriaan Kolff, Alter Domus (New York); Manuèle Biancarelli, NautaDutilh (Luxembourg); François Knaff, consul general; Thibaut Willems, NautaDutilh (New York); Jean-Marc Groelly, NautaDutilh (Luxembourg); 2008.

Patrizia Luchetta, Ministry of the Economy and Foreign Trade, 2008.

Cynthia Stroum, U.S. ambassador to Luxembourg (2009-).

E-commerce roundtable presenters Anne Murrath (PWC Luxembourg) and François-Xavier Dujardin (PWC New York), 2008.

Laurent Probst, PWC (Luxembourg), 2008.

Luxembourg: European Gateway for Islamic Finance breakfast seminar participants (left to right): François Knaff, consul general; Lawrence J. Blascovich, HSBC (New York); Toni Dudsak, executive director, LACC; Pierre Weimerskirch, Ernst & Young (Luxembourg); Germain Birgen, HSBC (Luxembourg); and Jacques Bofferding, Fortis Prime Fund Solutions (New York); 2009.

Luc Decker, Ministry of the Economy and Foreign Trade, 2008.

Ambassador Jean-Louis Wolzfeld and Boutros Boutros-Ghali, secretary general of the UN, February 4, 1993.

Ambassador Hubert Wurth and Kofi Annan, secretary general of the UN, August 5, 1998.

Ambassador Jean-Marc Hoscheit and Kofi Annan, secretary general of the UN, September 2, 2003.

Ambassador Sylvie Lucas and Ban Ki-moon, secretary general of the UN, August 25, 2008.

Consulate General of Luxembourg and Permanent Mission of Luxembourg to the United Nations

Receptions

Holiday gathering participants Hubert Wurth, ambassador to the UN, and his wife, Mrs. Francisca Passchier, 1998.

Reunion of Luxembourg's honorary consuls in the U.S., including (back row, left) Jean Graff, consul general; (back row, third from left) Alphonse Berns, Luxembourg ambassador to the U.S.; and (front row, third from right) Jacques F. Poos, minister of foreign affairs; 1996.

Celebratory reception for Luxembourg tennis champion Gilles Müller (center), U.S. Open quarterfinalist, 2008.

Reception with pianist Michel Reis. Left to right, front row: Patricia Feider and Anne Dostert, Permanent Mission; Michel Reis; back row: Véronique Olinger-Masquelin, Célir Mersch, Maïté Van der Vekene, Jean Olinger, and Adrien Vincentelli, Permanent Mission; 2009.

Luxembourg National Day Celebration. Left to right: Jacques E. Lennon, Luxembourg honorary consul in New York; Mrs. Donatella Lennon; Jean-Marc Hoscheit, ambassador to the UN; and Mrs. Nicole Hoscheit; 2008.

Cocktail reception for Jacques Santer, president of the European Commission. Left to right: Jean Graff, consul general and executive director, BED; Johny Lahure, minister of health and environment; Jacques Santer; Jean-Louis Wolzfeld, ambassador to the UN; and Danièle Santer; 1998.

H.R.H. Grand Duke Henri converses with architect I.M. Pei at a gala reception, 1999. A model of the architect's Musée d'Art Moderne Grand-Duc Jean (MUDAM) was featured in Famous Americans in Luxembourg: Art & Architecture, a 2008 exhibit.

Robert Brandy's paintings were exhibited in 2001 and 2003 (Jazz & Art exhibition).

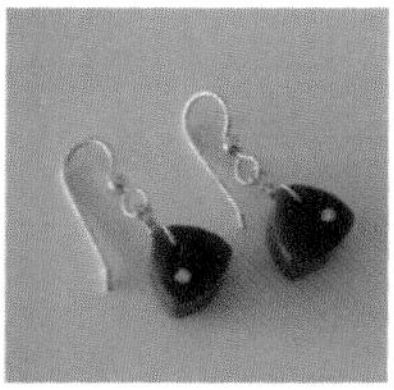

Jewelry designer Patrice Parisotto shows off her creations at the Elegance and Nature exhibit, 2008.

Calmes's Street Poetry.

Painter Elisabeth Calmes discusses her techniques with a guest at her While Meandering Through New York exhibit, 2008. Her first exhibit was Luxembourg – Paris – New York, 2006.

Creative Arts

Artists		Event	Country of Origin
Famous Americans in Luxembourg: Art & Architecture – Exhibition			
Arquitectonica	Architecture Firm	Banque de Luxembourg, 1994 – photo display	USA
Richard Meier	Architect	HypoVereinsbank, 1993 – model (courtesy of R. Meier)	USA
Iho Ming Pei	Architect	MUDAM – Museum of Modern Art, 2006 – model (courtesy MUDAM)	USA
Richard Serra	Architect & Painter	Exchange 1996 – photo/banner display of Serra's work by Raoul Sommers (Dutch) *Look into What, 2001*– painting (courtesy of Melva Bucksbaum and Raymond Learsy)	USA
Frank Stella	Architect & Painter	Sarreguemines 1993 – photo display *Ganji Dareh "F" Monoprint, 2001* – painting (courtesy of F. Stella)	USA
Michael Anton	Photographer	Jazz & Art – photo exhibit of Luxembourg's telecommunications and steel industries Music by Garlicks Jazz Quartet (Luxembourg)	USA
Robert Brandy	Author & Painter	Jazz & Art – Painting exhibition Music by Francesco T. Schlimé Jazz Quartet (Luxembourg)	Luxembourg
Elisabeth Calmes	Painter	Luxembourg – Paris – New York While Meandering through New York	Luxembourg
Ray Donarski	Painter	Exhibition	USA
Michèle Frank	Painter	Joint Exhibition	France–Luxembourg resident
René Wiroth	Sculptor		Luxembourg
Robert Hall Diane Jodes	Printers & Engravers	Revisiting Irving Berlin	USA Luxembourg
Vicky Hinger	Sculptor	Stonelegance	Luxembourg
Roseline Koener	Painter	Textures of Joy	Luxembourg

Artists		Event	Country of Origin
Danièle-Christine Kremer	Jewelry creator	Business Abstract	Luxembourg
Yvon Lambert	Photographer	New York Chronicles	Luxembourg
Philippe Lamesch	Printmaker	New Territory	Luxembourg
Josiane Marschal	Painter	De Klenge Roude Punkt	Luxembourg
Michel Medinger	Photographer	Strange Parade	Luxembourg
Iva Mzarkova	Painter	Illustrations for ***Portraits de Femmes Célèbres Luxembourgeoises***, a book by Luxembourg author and editor Katja Rausch (Luxembourg)	Czech Republic – Luxembourg resident
Patrice Parisotto Véronique Rischard	Jewelry Creator Painter	Elegance and Nature	Luxembourg Luxembourg
Lucile Risch	Photographer	You Won't Escape My Love	Luxembourg
David Russon	Painter	Exhibition	Luxembourg
Françoise-Marie Thein	Sculptor	Exhibition	Luxembourg
Ann Vinck	Painter	Painting & Woodcut	Luxembourg
Tom Wagener	Painter	Coup de Cœur	Luxembourg
Marc Weydert	Photographer	New York Through a Lens	Luxembourg
Wade Zimmerman	Photographer	Luxembourg City: Capital of Culture 2007 – photo exhibition including Salle de Concerts Grande-Duchesse Joséphine-Charlotte, home of the Luxembourg Philharmonic Orchestra	USA

Dance

Director

Li Marteling of Li Marteling Dance Studio (Luxembourg)

Choreographers and teachers of *Just Dancing 2007*

Li Marteling

Manoel Batistar	Paola Commisso	Elizabeth Dury

Presentation of *Just Dancing 2007* at Turtle Bay Music School by these Luxembourg dancers

Jessica Bausch	Véronique Baustert	Mona Biwer
Lena Bodeving	Lisa Breyer	Chloé Chrétien
Lis Dahm	Myriam Decker	Maïté Drees
Axelle Feider	Jil Fischer	Lynn Friedrich
Julie Freylinger	Caroline Glesener	Annick Hemmerling
Lynn Hendriks	Kelly Janizzi	Enja Jans
Jil Jelsma	Julie Kayser	Linda Kieffer
Anne Klensch	Alexandra Kohl	Céline Kolb
Jenna Krings	Catherine Leidner	Jackie Ley,
Anne-Catherine Loesch	Anne-Sophie Loos	Deborah Lotti
Maïté Margue	Ornella Mastrangelo	Nina May
Cathy Moes	Carole Munhowen	Kelly Niesen
Marie Prüm	Cynthia Rafael	Stefania Rossi
Sally Sandt	Julie Schadeck	Caroline Schartz
Noémie Schintgen	Annick Schlesser	Lis Schroeder
Rebecca Sinclair	Jil Streber	Nathalie Tondt
Susanna Tron	Vanessa Wagner	Anne Wies
Isabelle Wildgen		

Curtis Roosevelt, grandson of President Franklin D. Roosevelt (left), at a signing for his book *Too Close to the Sun,* with John Colligan, World War II veteran of the U.S. Fifth Armored Division, who participated in Luxembourg's 1944 liberation, 2009.

Edmond Israel signs a copy of his book *In Love with Life: An American Dream of a Luxembourger* for Georges Faber, consul general, 2006.

Li Marteling Dance Studio students receive applause for their performance of *Just Dancing, 2007* at the Turtle Bay Music School. Front row: choreographers Li Marteling and Elisabeth Dury with Consul General Georges Faber, 2007.

Katja Rausch (above right), author and editor of *Portraits de Femmes Célèbres Luxembourgeoises*, with book illustrator Iva Mrazkova (above left), attend a book signing and illustration exhibit in their honor, 2008.

A group of children including Alex (inset) and Michel (second from left) Knaff enjoy a screening of *Sinbad, Legend of the Seven Seas*, 2008. Luxembourger Tanja Majerus designed some of the film's animated characters.

Films

Film	Filmmakers	Country of Origin
Sinbad, Legend of the Seven Seas Animated Film	Tanja Majerus, animated characters designer	Luxembourg
Call Her Madam: Perle Mesta in Luxembourg Documentary	Paul Lesch, Director – Samsa Film Claude Waringo, Producer – Samsa Film Jani Thiltges, Producer – Samsa Film Co-Production, CNA (Centre National de l'Audiovisuel)	Luxembourg Luxembourg Luxembourg Luxembourg
Centre Culturel de Rencontre (CCR) Abbaye de Neumünster Documentary & Conference	Men Bodson, Producer Romain Goerend, Producer Claude Frisoni, General Manager of the CCR	Luxembourg Luxembourg Luxembourg
Léif Lëtzebuerger – Charlotte: A Royal at War Documentary	Ray Tostevin, Director – Grace Productions Candice Allen-Olson, Creator & Producer – Grace Productions Lynn Rothwell, Co-Producer – Grace Productions Joy Hoffmann, Co-Producer – CNA (Centre National de Luxembourg l'Audiovisuel) Curtis Roosevelt, grandson of President Franklin Delano Roosevelt and interviewee John Colligan, World War II veteran of the U.S. Fifth Armored Division and interviewee	UK Luxembourg Ireland USA USA USA
Luxembourg, USA Documentary	Willy Perlsztejn, Original idea & Producer – CNA (Centre National de l'Audiovisuel) Christophe Wagner, Director & Author – CNA	Luxembourg Luxembourg
Shades of Jazz on Noir Series: "La Femme Fatale" Film	Ana Isabel Ordonez, Writer and Filmmaker Music by The Ernie Hammes Lip Kill Trio featuring Ernie Hammes, trumpets (Luxembourg); Jay Anderson, bass (USA); and Jay Rosen, drums (USA)	French-Luxembourg resident

Literature, History And Sciences

Artists & Presenters		Event	Country of Origin
Robert Brandy	Author & Painter	Book Signing: *Robert Brandy's Studio* and painting exhibition	Luxembourg
Christian Dupont	Presenter	Conference regarding the book: *Hugo Gernsback: The Father of*	Luxembourg
Paul Lesch	Presenter	*Modern Science Fiction*	Luxembourg
Edmond Israel	Author	Book signing: *In Love with Life*	Luxembourg
Paul Lesch	Author & Historian	Book signing: *Playing Her Part: Perle Mesta in Luxembourg*	Luxembourg
David Leopold	Author	Book signing: *Irving Berlin's Show Business*	USA
Katja Rausch	Author & Editor	Book signing: *Portraits de Femmes Célèbres Luxembourgeoises* Illustrations by Iva Mzarkova (Czech–Luxembourg resident)	Luxembourg
Curtis Roosevelt	Author	Book signing: *Too Close to the Sun: Growing up in the Shadow of My Grandparents, Franklin and Eleanor*	USA
Lonnie D. Story	Author	Book signing: *The Meeting of Anni Adams: The Butterfly of Luxembourg*	USA

Music

Groups or Events	Musicians	Instruments	Country of Origin
Cello-loops	André Mergenthaler	Cello	Luxembourg
Chorale Grand Ducale	Jean Gehlen	Conductor	Luxembourg
Sainte Cécile de Wormeldange	Luc Rollinger	Organist	Luxembourg
	Anne Berna	Soprano	Luxembourg
	Danielle Bomb	Soprano	Luxembourg
	Josée Duhr	Soprano	Luxembourg
	Jeanny Pundel	Soprano	Luxembourg
	Marlies Theves	Soprano	Luxembourg
	Sonny Thorn	Soprano	Luxembourg
	Reiny Zoller	Soprano	Luxembourg
	Lynn Beining	Alto	Luxembourg
	Fabienne Lenert	Alto	Luxembourg
	Andrée Mathes	Alto	Luxembourg
	Lynn Schumacher	Alto	Luxembourg
	Joël Meyers	Tenor	Luxembourg
	Raymond Peters	Tenor	Luxembourg
	Jean-Marie Sadler	Tenor	Luxembourg
	Henri Schumacher	Tenor	Luxembourg
	Raymond Berna	Bass	Luxembourg
	Pierre Reding	Bass	Luxembourg
	Luc Schumacher	Bass	Luxembourg
	Patrick Waldbillig	Bass	Luxembourg
Dream Catcher – Pop-Rock Band	John Rech	Vocals	Luxembourg
	Eric Falchero	Piano	Luxembourg
	Remo Cavallini	Guitar	Luxembourg
	Christian Harpes	Bass	Luxembourg
	Joel Heyard	Drums	Luxembourg
Francesco Tristano Schlimé	Francesco Tristano Schlimé	Piano	Luxembourg
Classical Music Duet	Johnny Gandelsman	Violin	Russia
	Justin Messina	Composer	USA

Groups or Events	Musicians	Instruments	Country of Origin
Francesco Tristano Schlimé Jazz/Brazilian Duet	Francesco Tristano Schlimé	Piano	Luxembourg
	Raimundo Penaforte	Violin & Percussion	Brazil
Francesco Tristano Schlimé Jazz Quartet	Francesco Tristano Schlimé	Piano	Luxembourg
	Jérôme Goldschmidt	Percussion	Luxembourg
	Paul Wiltgen	Drums	Luxembourg
	William Perry Wortman	Bass	USA
Garlicks Jazz Quartet	Jitz Jeitz	Saxophone	Luxembourg
	Al Lenners	Drums	Luxembourg
	John Schlammes	Bass	Luxembourg
	Georges Urwald	Piano	Luxembourg
Greg Lamy Jazz Quartet	Greg Lamy	Guitar	USA–Luxembourg resident
	Gretchen Parlato	Vocals	USA
	Massimo Biolcati	Bass	USA
	Javier Vercher	Saxophone	Spain
	Ferenc Nemeth	Drums	Hungary
Jean Muller Classical Solo Recital	Jean Muller	Piano	Luxembourg
Jérôme Goldschmidt Latin Jazz Sextet	Jérôme Goldschmidt	Percussion	Luxembourg
	Oscar Hernandez	Piano	USA
	John Walsh	Trumpets	Germany
	Gregor Huebner	Violin	USA
	Ruben Rodriguez	Bass	USA & Puerto Rico
	Jotan Afanador	Drums	USA & Puerto Rico
Marc Demuth Jazz Quartet	Marc Demuth	Bass	Luxembourg
	Sofia Ribeiro	Vocals	Portugal
	Pascal Schumacher	Vibraphone	Luxembourg
	Joachim Badenhorst	Clarinet	Belgium
	Yves Peeters	Drums	Belgium
Martin Reuter Jazz Trio	Martin Reuter	Drums	Luxembourg
	Joe Young	Guitar	USA
	Radu Ben Judah	Bass	USA

Music *(continued)*

Groups or Events	Musicians	Instruments	Country of Origin
Maxime Bender Jazz Quartet featuring Will Vinson	Maxime Bender	Saxophone	Luxembourg
	Sebastian Sternal	Piano	Germany
	Markus Braun	Bass	Germany
	Silvio Morger	Drums	Switzerland
	Will Vinson	Saxophone	UK
Michel Reis Jazz Trio	Michel Reis	Piano	Luxembourg
	Michael Oien	Bass	USA
	Eric Doob	Drums	USA
Paul Wiltgen Jazz Trio	Paul Wiltgen	Drums/Composer/Band Leader	Luxembourg
	Michel Reis	Piano	Luxembourg
	Aidan Carroll	Bass	USA
Songs from *Call Me Madam* (First Irving Berlin Salon Series)	Vira Slywotzky	Opera Singer (soprano)	USA
	Ricardo Rivera	Opera Singer (baritone)	USA
	Andrew Osarchuk	Opera Singer (tenor)	USA
	Heidi Sauser	Opera Singer (soprano)	USA
	Ted Taylor	Musical Director/Piano	USA
	Ted Chapin	Narrator	USA
The Ernie Hammes Group	Ernie Hammes	Trumpets	Luxembourg
	Frank Spaniol	Saxophone	Germany
	Pierre-Alain Goualch	Piano	France
	Diégo Imbert	Bass	France
	Oliver Strauch	Drums	Germany
The Ernie Hammes Lip Kill Trio	Ernie Hammes	Trumpets	Luxembourg
	Jay Anderson	Bass	USA
	Jay Rosen	Drums	USA
Troaterbattien	Robert Koeller	Conductor	Luxembourg
		Brass Band (30 musicians)	Luxembourg
Friends of Irving Berlin	John Wallowitch	40/50 professionals and amateurs singing Berlin's compositions	USA
We Hymn "White Christmas"	Bobb Goldsteinn		USA
"White Christmas" at the Luxembourg House (Second Irving Berlin Salon Series)	Glory Crampton	Broadway performer (soprano)	USA
	Kevin Early	Broadway performer (baritone)	USA
	Ross Patterson	Piano	USA

The Troaterbattien brass band, led by Robert Koeller, plays on National Day on Beekman Place's cul-de-sac, 2005.

Paul Wiltgen—jazz drummer, composer, and band leader—played with the Francesco Tristano Schlimé Jazz Quartet, 2003.

he Jérôme Goldschmidt Latin Jazz Sextet performs in elebration of their tenth anniversary (left to right): Oscar ernandez (keyboard), Ruben Rodriguez (bass), Jérôme oldschmidt (percussion), John Walsh (trumpet), Jotan Afanador lrums, behind Walsh), and Gregor Huebner (violin), 2006.

The Chorale Grand Ducale Sainte Cécile de Wormeldange sings in the terrace garden following a performance at St. Patrick's Cathedral, 2010.

laxime Bender Jazz Quartet plays improvisational vorks (left to right): Sebastian Sternal (keyboard), larkus Braun (bass), Will Vinson (alto saxophone), Silvio lorger (drums, behind Vinson), and Maxime Bender enor and soprano saxophones), 2010.

Jay Anderson, bass player for the Ernie Hammes Lip Kill Trio, performs during the "La Femme Fatale" *Shades of Jazz on Noir* Series, 2009.

The Marc Demuth Jazz Quartet performs in honor of the Francophonie Festival in New York. Sofia Ribeiro (featured singer), and Marc Demuth (bass player), 2005.

Clay Constantinou, U.S. ambassador to Luxembourg (1994-1999), 2009.

James V. Forrestal's daughter-in-law, Katherine (Kit) Callahan Forrestal (widow of Peter Forrestal), and her daughter, Francesca Forrestal, 2010.

Marianne Lehners, 2010.

Luxembourgers (left to right): Joséphine Krieger, Nadine Seltzer, Annie Harris-Wagner, and Adeline Seltzer with George Wagner, c. 1995.

James M. Barquinero, Sacred Heart University and LACC, 2008.

Maud Reiter, LACC, 2009.

Fiona McKenzie, UNICEF, and Elizabeth Daly, director/international business, New York City Commission for the UN; 2009.

Marc Mergen and his wife, Elaine Chu.

Georges Jacquemart, 2009.

Left to right: Saba Amroun-Febres, Consulate General; Isabelle Strong, Laurence Waucampt, and Magali Guerbi, Permanent Mission; Tatjana Schaefer, executive director, LACC; Jerry Seeman, Luxcore; Megan McGough, LACC; 2010. Not shown: Soumaya Bellamine.

Laurence Pierron, TIO (New York), and Josée Deroy, HSBC (New York), at a reception, 2008.

Stan Myck and Marc Bichler, Permanent Mission, 2005.

Annie Bastian, director, Luxembourg Tourist Office, 1991.

Left to right: Philippe Donckel, Antoine Bernardy, Véronique Dockendorf, and Marc Weydert, Permanent Mission; 2010.

Léo Faber and Olivier Maes, Permanent Mission; 2010.

ACKNOWLEDGMENTS

PROLOGUE AND CHAPTER ONE

The author extends gratitude to the following organizations and institutions and their staff members:

PROLOGUE: THE ELITE LEGACY OF BEEKMAN PLACE

New-York Historical Society: Susan Kriete and Jill Slaight; Office for Metropolitan History: Christopher Gray.

CHAPTER ONE: THE FORRESTAL YEARS, 1929-1946

Department of Finance, Manhattan City Register: Dennis Nesmith; City of New York Department of Records & Information Services, Municipal Archives: Leonora Gidlund; Columbia University, Avery Architectural & Fine Arts Library: Janet Parks; Estate of Yousuf Karsh: Julie Grahame; The Frick Art Reference Library: Anna Cavado and Suz Massen; Goucher College: Stuart Meck, FAICP/PP, faculty, Master of Arts in Historic Preservation Program, and Nancy Magnuson, librarian, and the 2006 Julia Rogers Research Prize Committee; The Metropolitan Museum of Art, Thomas J. Watson Library: Lisa Harns; New York City Department of Buildings: Angela Orridge; New-York Historical Society: Susan Kriete and Jill Slaight; Museum of the City of New York: Robbi Siegel; New York Public Library, Art and Architecture Collection: Ryan Haley; Princeton University, Mudd Manuscript Library, James V. Forrestal Papers (1907-1958): Adrien Hanson and Christine Lutz; Smithsonian Institution Archives of American Art, Harold Sterner Papers, 1929-1978: Wendy Hurlock Baker and Margaret Zoller.

Special thanks to Katherine (Kit) Callahan Forrestal, widow of Peter Forrestal, for her avid interest in my work and generosity of time, materials, and information; and to Francesca Forrestal, her daughter, who connected us. Additional appreciation goes to Millicent Ogden McKinley Cox and to Mrs. Nancy Streeter, granddaughter of Ellen Biddle Shipman, for their kind contributions of photographs.

CHAPTER TWO: THE BERLIN YEARS, 1947-1989

The author expresses sincere appreciation to the daughters of Irving Berlin—Mary Ellin Barrett, Linda Emmet, and Elizabeth Peters—for their interest in the project and kindness in sharing recollections of 17 Beekman Place during the years the family lived there. Without their vivid memories of the furnishings, decoration, artwork, and the family's lifestyle in the house, the story of the Berlin years on Beekman Place could not have been written. They were very generous with their time, for which the author is truly grateful.

In addition, thanks go to Bert Fink and Carol Cornicelli of Rodgers & Hammerstein: An Imagem Company, which represents the Irving Berlin Music Company, for assistance in gathering information on Mr. Berlin's career, and in collecting photographs and illustrations to accompany the story.

Others, too, contributed to the project. Among them: Michael Miscione, borough historian of Manhattan; Michael Kerker, American Society of Composers, Authors and Publishers; Raymond White, Music Division of the Library of Congress; David Kirkland, Steinway and Sons; and Pamela Cruz, Girl Scouts of the USA.

CHAPTER THREE: THE LUXEMBOURG YEARS, 1990-PRESENT

The author extends heartfelt thanks to Edward W. Emmet, grandson of Ellin and Irving Berlin, for sharing his personal memories; Michel Franck, AIA, managing principal, Spacesmith, for his professional expertise and extensive input regarding the renovation of the house; and, Jerrold S. Seeman, Esq., chief executive officer, Luxcore, Ltd., for his input and guidance concerning the activities of the Trade and Investment Office.

In addition, the author is most grateful to the following individuals employed with the Luxembourg government for their time and input on this project: Saba Amroun-Febres, executive assistant to the consul general; Toni Dudsak, former director,

Luxembourg American Chamber of Commerce; Brigitte Goergen, director, Luxembourg National Tourist Office; François Knaff, consul general and executive director of the Trade and Investment Office; Ambassador Sylvie Lucas, permanent representative of Luxembourg to the United Nations; Jean Olinger, deputy permanent representative of the Mission; and Laurence Pierron, executive assistant to the executive director of the TIO.

Notes

Prologue: The Elite Legacy of Beekman Place

7 A short section of Forty-ninth Street east of First Avenue became Mitchell Place in 1871. Mitchell, a lawyer and judge, was a descendant of Peter Anderson, to whom the Dutch West India Company granted land in Turtle Bay in 1645. (Sanna Feirstein, *Naming New York: Manhattan Places & How They Got Their Names*, 114.)

7 The area that…two Englishmen: Carol von Pressentin Wright, *Blue Guide: New York*, 339; reaching from…Forty-ninth streets: Edmund T. Delaney, *New York's Turtle Bay, Old & New*, 14.

7 Beginning as early as 1712: "Turtle Bay:" Harmon H. Goldstone and Martha Dalrymple, *History Preserved: A Guide to New York City Landmarks and Historic Districts*, 239; perhaps because…the bay: Jerry Cheslow, "If You're Thinking of Living in Turtle Bay," *New York Times (NYT)*, Apr. 26, 1992; or…turtle population: Delaney, 2.

7 Turtle Bay began to play: Ibid., 3.

8 In 1868, its little bay: Ibid., 17.

8 Beekman Place was carved: Ibid., 4.

8 James Beekman, a prominent patriot: "The Old Beekman Mansion," *NYT*, May 23, 1874.

8 initially located: Atlases of New York City, Maps of farms commonly called the *Blue Book* – 1815, image 1531811 [Sakersdorff Farm Set, 1868], NYPL Digital Gallery Web site, Sept. 1, 2009, http://www.digitalgallery.nypl.org/.

8 its greenhouse was the scene…Nathan Hale: Delaney, 7; "a spy and traitor…": Wright, 339.

8 when Fifty-first Street opened: "Demolition of the Beekman House," *NYT*, May 27, 1874; mansion was moved: date from "History," Turtle Bay Association Web site, Sept. 5, 2009, http://www.turtlebay-nyc.org/; at great expense: Philip L. White, *The Beekmans of New York in Politics and Commerce, 1647-1877*, 618.

8 In 1854, Beekman vacated…Switzerland: White, 618; conditions around…moved north: Pamela Hanlon, *Manhattan's Turtle Bay: Story of a Midtown Neighborhood*, 19. In summer 1854, 2,509 died of cholera in New York City. (John Macpherson, *Epidemic Cholera: Its Mission and Mystery, Haunts and Havocs, Pathology and Treatments*, 112.) Beekman's daughter remained in New York to attend school.

9 While he was away: White, 618-619.

9 Returning to New York…5 East 34th Street: Trow's New York City Directory, 1857-58, "James W. Beekman."

9 From 1864 to 1866: *Record of Assessment, Manhattan, 19th Ward, 1864 (I)*, 75, 79, and *Record of Assessment, Manhattan, 19th Ward, 1866 (II)*, 83-85, City of New York Department of Finance, Manhattan City Register.

9 In 1865, Samuel W. Dunscomb: Ibid.

9 As a condition of purchase…Fiftieth Street: "Old Restriction on Part of Famous Beekman Farm Prevents Improvement of Two River Front Blocks," *NYT*, Dec. 5, 1914; "dangerous, noxious, or offensive": Irini Sarlis, "Another Endangered Neighborhood," *Oculus 46, No. 3* (May 1985): 22. Fiftieth Street in the Beekman Place enclave was originally "Dunscomb Place."

9 In return, Dunscomb erected: "Old Restriction…"

9 The intimate layout: Paul Goldberger, "Explorer's Guide to Manhattan's Hidden Places," *NYT*, Dec. 5, 1980. Other New York enclaves (approximately twenty) are comprised of dwellings set around a square, converted carriage houses, or multiple-occupancy dwellings built specifically for the working classes.

9 Brownstone, a form of sandstone: Charles Lockwood, *Bricks and Brownstone: The New York Row House, 1783-1929*, 139, 141.

10 According to early directories: Christopher Gray, "Streetscapes/Beekman Place; A Two-Block Street Down by the East Riverside," *NYT*, Nov. 30, 1997.

10 Dunscomb lived in Mount Pleasant: "The Rev. Samuel W. Dunscomb," Obituaries, *NYT*, Apr. 3, 1902.

10 no longer listed: *Record of Assessment, Manhattan, 19th Ward, 1868 (I)*, 82-85, City of New York Department of Finance, Manhattan City Register.

10 The grand mansion's 1874 demise: Michael Freitag, "If You're Thinking of Living in Beekman Place," *NYT*, Aug. 24, 1986.

10 James Beekman died: "Realty Trials of Beekman Estate," *NYT*, Feb. 29, 1920.

10 Soon, the area along the bank: Delaney, 21.

10 Flanked by…the north: Christopher Gray, "A Two Block Street Down by the East Riverside," *NYT*, Nov. 30, 1997; Beekman Place's… boarding houses: Gray, "Streetscapes/Beekman Place…."

10 In 1919, renowned landscape architect: Ibid; comprising her…apartments: Cynthia Zaitzevsky, *Long Island Landscapes and the Women Who Designed Them*, 11. Today, this house is Nos. 19-21.

10 In 1922, the Beekman family: generally, Christopher Gray, "Streetscapes/1 Beekman Place; A Rockefeller Co-op and Its 460-Foot-Long Garage," *NYT*, Oct. 1, 2000.

11 The Beekman Hill Association: Edited by Kenneth T. Jackson, *The Encyclopedia of New York City* (Yale University Press, New Haven & London, 1995), 96. The Beekman Place Association was founded in 1980 for the security, preservation, and beautification of Beekman Place.

11 the 1924…Beekman Terrace: New York Building Information System (BIS) Web site, Sept. 6, 2009, http://www.bisweb.nyc.gov/, Certificate of Occupancy No. 9043, Dec. 31, 1924; the 1928 Panhellenic Tower: Ibid, Certificate of Occupancy No. 143417, Aug. 30, 1928. The Panhellenic Tower, now the Beekman Tower Hotel, was designated a New York City Landmark in 1998.

Chapter One: The Forrestal Years, 1929-1946

POSTSCRIPT

James V. Forrestal left his post as U.S. Secretary of Defense in March 1949. Tragically, he died two months later, on May 22, as the result of a fall from a window at Bethesda Naval Hospital outside Washington, D.C., where he was being treated for depression. Forrestal received numerous posthumous honors. In 1954, the Navy introduced the Forrestal-class of aircraft carriers, christening one of them the U.S.S. Forrestal. Princeton University named two facilities for him: the 1952 James Forrestal Research Center, dedicated largely to aerospace and mechanical sciences research, and the 1975 Princeton Forrestal Center, a corporate office and research park. And the U.S. Department of Energy headquarters in Washington became the Forrestal Building.

Jo Forrestal moved to Paris during World War II, later settling in Newport. She died in 1976. Michael and Peter both attended Princeton, but only Peter graduated from the school. Michael went on to obtain a law degree from Harvard University and became an international relations specialist. He died in 1989. Peter, an investment banker who worked for Dillon, Read for a time, died in 1982, just eight months after his marriage to Kit Callahan. Several months later, their daughter Francesca, the Forrestals' only grandchild, was born. Jim, Jo, Michael, and Peter Forrestal are buried in Section 30 of Arlington National Cemetery in Arlington, Virginia.

(Sources: generally, Hoopes and Brinkley; Princeton University Web Site; Princeton Forrestal Center Web site; and Kit Forrestal conversations with author, fall 2009.)

Unless otherwise noted: Descriptions of the exterior details of 17 Beekman Place are based on the author's observations. Descriptions of the interiors of the house are from the Harold Sterner Papers, 1929-1978, Archives of American Art, Smithsonian Institution; unidentified interior design publication, c.1930s, 33-36.

13 dominating the financial…consumerism: Carl Abbott, *Urban America in the Modern Age*, 12; Wall Street was: Townsend Hoopes and Douglas Brinkley, *Driven Patriot: The Life and Times of James Forrestal*, 27.

14 New York was most affected: Edward Robb Ellis, *The Epic of New York City: A Narrative History*, 533, 551.
14 By 1930, a quarter of its office space: Laurence Gerkens, *The Shaping of the American City*, D-4.
14 By the end of 1932: Ellis, 533, 551.
14 Nationally, the unemployment figure: Gerkens, F-1.
14 one of the era's "golden boys": Hoopes and Brinkley, 61.
14 Forrestal married: "Miss Ruth Fargeon Weds J.Q. Rowling," *New York Times* (*NYT*), Oct. 14, 1926; the year: "Manhattan Private Home Plans at Low Record," *NYT*, Feb. 9, 1930.
14 Jo was living at Beekman Mansion: "Miss Ruth Fargeon..." Located at 439 East Fifty-first Street, the building was designed by Van Wart & Wein and Treanor & Fatio and completed in 1926. (Robert A.M. Stern, Gregory Gilmartin, and Thomas Mellins, *New York 1930: Architecture and Urbanism Between the Two World Wars*, 433.)
14 Initially, the newlyweds lived: Hoopes and Brinkley, 46.
14 the Forrestals rented...June 4, 1928 they purchased: *Register - New York County Abstract Index - U.S., W.P.A.*, Block 1361, Section 5, 1-34; 000169, citation C7825, City of New York Department of Finance, Manhattan City Register.
14 A building permit was filed: New York Building Information System (BIS) Web site, Sept. 6, 2009, Certificate of Occupancy No. 18219, Feb. 13, 1932, Bureau of Buildings, Borough of Manhattan, City of New York, http://www.bisweb.nyc.gov/.
14 Forrestal viewed construction: Hoopes and Brinkley, 83.
15 Seventeen Beekman Place was one of the last: "Manhattan Private Home..."
16 his net worth: Hoopes and Brinkley, 83.
16 often called...boyhood: Ibid., 9.
16 The last of three...punitive mother: Arnold A. Rogow, *James Forrestal: A Study of Personality, Politics and Policy*, 50-52.
16 While only about...height: Hoopes and Brinkley, 14.
16 His father...between them: Rogow, 61-62.
16 In high school: Hoopes and Brinkley, 15-16.
16 After his 1908 graduation: Ibid., 16-20.
16 One year later: Rogow, 58, 60.
16 Less privileged...*Daily Princetonian*: Hoopes and Brinkley, 21.
17 Forrestal left Princeton...determined to reverse: Ibid., 28 and Rogow, 64.
17 after initial employment...December 1919: Rogow, 65-68.
17 its largest city began attracting: Stern, Gilmartin, and Mellins, 15.
17 returning to Dillon, Read: Rogow, 66.
17 Forrestal was...proper circles: Hoopes and Brinkley, generally, 22-26, 38.
17 Josephine Ogden Forrestal...back to Chicago: Ibid., 43.
17 Jo inherited...the city: Ibid.
18 Establishing herself...in the crowd: Ibid., 43-44.
18 It is believed...marry her new love: Ibid., 44-45.
18 Around the same time: Ibid., 45.
18 She would leave her position: "Miss Ruth Fargeon..."
18 Jo and Jim married: Ibid; over time: Hoopes and Brinkley, 46.
19 in the late 1920s...1820 manor house: Ibid., 75. The estate was purchased on February 2, 1929.
19 Clarence Dillon: Ibid., 70-73.
19 Forrestal reaped the rewards: Ibid., 55-61. Dillon, Read bought Dodge Brothers, a prominent yet stagnating automotive company, for a record-setting cash transaction of $146 million in 1925, then sold it to Chrysler Corporation in 1928. (Charles K. Hyde, *The Dodge Brothers: The Men, the Motor Cars, and the Legacy*, 178, 203.)
19 Finally, he created: Ibid., 70-73.
19 Forrestal commissioned: Hoopes and Brinkley, 83.
19 the 1930 One Beekman Place: Gray, "Streetscapes/1 Beekman Place...."; the 1931 Two Beekman Place: New York Building Information System (BIS) Web site, Sept. 10, 2009, Certificate of Occupancy No. 17824, Sept. 11, 1931.
19 The city widened...guardrails: "Beekman Place to Be Repaved," *NYT*, Nov. 2, 1930.
19 settled in 1932: New York Building Information System (BIS) Web site, Sept. 10, 2009, Certificate of Occupancy No. 18219.
20 6,426 gross square feet...20-by-100-foot lot:

calculations by Terry Hudak, Nov. 30, 2009.

21 Between the World Wars…American aesthetics: generally, Mark Gelernter, *A History of American Architecture: Buildings in Their Cultural and Technological Context*, 231-234. Georgian architecture…eighteenth-century: Cyril M. Harris, ed., Illustrated Dictionary of Historic Architecture, 249.

22 "baby skyscraper": unidentified interior design publication, c.1930s, 33.

22 which reflects the domination: Gelernter, 75.

22 A second entry: Michel Franck, AIA, managing principal, Spacesmith; former principal, Michel Franck Architect PC, architect of record for the Luxembourg Government's renovation of 17 Beekman Place; email message, April 4, 2009.

24 fronted the entrance foyer's: Linda (Berlin) Emmet, conversation with co-author Hanlon, Sept. 2009.

24 The decorating firm…classical accents: *Zenitherm: For Walls and Floors* brochure, Jones & Erwin office photograph, 1930, 12. The firm's address was 15 East Fifty-seventh Street.

24 The Forrestals' custom elevator was manufactured by Gurney Elevators of New York.

25 Forrestal's favorite room…cigars: Hoopes and Brinkley, 83.

25 The Smallpox Hospital became the Home for the Nurses of the Maternity and City Hospital Training School in 1875. Renwick also designed New York's St. Patrick's Cathedral (1858).

25 fireplace, which originally had: Luxembourg Consulate of New York, renovation photographs, 1990.

26 Robert Adam was an eighteenth century Scottish Neo-Classical architect, interior designer, and furniture designer.

26 The door frame's…view: author's observations.

27 Curved floor-to-ceiling…decorating opportunities: author's observations.

27 "somewhat modernistic": "Manhattan Private Home…"

27 an opulent bed: Hoopes and Brinkley, 84.

28 had marble fixtures…fireplace surround: Linda (Berlin) Emmet, conversation with co-author Hanlon, Nov. 2009, and Luxembourg Consulate of New York, renovation photographs, 1990.

28 Jim Forrestal's bedroom-study…luxury liner: generally, Hoopes and Brinkley, 84.

29 Forrestal boxed…physique: Rogow, 55; a favorite Bellows: Hoopes and Brinkley, 84.

29 At their Long Island estate: Ibid., 76.

29 a central calling system: Franck.

29 The fifth floor: "Manhattan Private Home…"

29 It comprised a bedroom…to the east: Mary Ellin (Berlin) Barrett, conversation with co-author Hanlon, Aug. 2009.

30 "creative" and "knew how to make a house interesting": Hoopes and Brinkley, 76.

30 Seeking drama…decorative additions, generally: Ibid., 84.

30 Jo was meticulous: Ibid., 77.

30 Jo had a particular affinity: Katharine (Kit) Callahan Forrestal (Peter Forrestal's widow), conversation with author, Nov. 10, 2009.

30 insisting on custom-made: Rogow, 70, and Hoopes and Brinkley, 39.

31 Perhaps their most extravagant…the minuet: "Pomp of Bourbons Seen in Opera Ball," *NYT*, Apr. 28, 1934.

31 In 1935…Cecil Beaton: "J.V. Forrestals Hosts," *NYT*, Mar. 26, 1935.

31 In 1936: "Miss Julia Berwind Hostess at Newport," *NYT*, June 29, 1936.

31 The Forrestals also traveled…chic locales: Hoopes and Brinkley, 86.

31 Jim was a trustee…frail as a child: Rogow, 55.

32 Among the many worthy causes: "Leading the Way in Social Activities for Charities," *NYT*, Dec. 16, 1934.

33 Their father, who was stingy: generally, Hoopes and Brinkley, 88.

33 While Forrestal was at least: Ibid., 94.

34 Jo was only slightly: Ibid.,89.

34 The boys most often dined: Rogow, 75.

34 There, their father: Ibid., 74, 76.

34 Forrestal was conscious…weekends: Hoopes and Brinkley, 88.

34 When Michael was…Switzerland: Rogow, 77; returned…World War II: Kit Forrestal conversation.

34 Eventually, Jo enrolled…happy there: Hoopes and Brinkley, 91.

35 Early that year...service in the government: Rogow, 89.
35 welcome an opportunity: Ibid., 90.
35 paid $10,000 a year: Ibid.
35 Jo, anticipating: Hoopes and Brinkley, 118.
35 moved out of their Beekman Place residence: In Washington, D.C., the Forrestals lived at Prospect House at 3508 Prospect Avenue, listed on the National Register of Historic Places. (Washington, D.C.: A National Register of Historic Places Travel Itinerary, "Georgetown Historic District," Dec. 28, 2009, www.nps.gov/nr/travel/wash/dc15.htm.)
35 Forrestal assumed his job: Hoopes and Brinkley, 122.
35 with the critical job of: Ibid., 163-164.
36 "plan[ned] to take back the house that autumn [1945]": Princeton University, Seeley G. Mudd Manuscript Library, James V. Forrestal Papers, 1907-1958 (bulk 1940-1949), Box 92, Folder 16; James Forrestal letter to Daniel Arnstein, July 14, 1945.
36 "convert the house into a rooming house for paying guests": Princeton University, Daniel Arnstein letter to James Forrestal, Aug. 3, 1945.
36 When Forrestal finally decided to sell: Hoopes and Brinkley, 245.

SIDEBARS

Harold Sterner, the Forrestals' Architect

20 lived close to Beekman Place: New York City Telephone Directory, Manhattan White Pages, Winter 1932-Summer 1933, NYPL, reel 3. Sterner purchased this four-story brownstone apartment house in March 1929, seven months before the stock market crashed. ("Bing & Bing to Build Flat in Yorkville," *NYT*, Mar. 15, 1929.)
20 Born in Paris...1895: Harold Sterner, U.S. World War II Draft Registration Card, 1942, Roll WW2_2368823; he was the son...1917: Christine M. Miles, compiled by. Goodrich, Lloyd and Michael Sterner, introduction. Harold Sterner: *Architect & Artist, A Retrospective of His Work – April 1-June 15, 1978.*
20 In 1923...Edmond L. Knoedler: "Social Notes," *NYT*, April 29, 1923. Marie Sterner worked at Knoedler Gallery before later establishing her own.
20 would go on to have: "The Political Graveyard: Index to Politicians," Political Graveyard, September 21, 2009. http://www.politicalgraveyard.com/.
20 Sterner worked for: New York City Telephone Directory, Manhattan White Pages, Winter 1932-Summer 1933, NYPL, reel 3. The firm was later Pennington, Lewis & Mills.
20 He was...junior member: Miles, compiled by. "Record of Principal Work Executed by Harold Sterner"; in 1926: Ibid. and Gray, "Streetscapes/Beekman Place"; a $300,000 renovation: "Record of Principal Work Executed by Harold Sterner," Harold Sterner Papers, 1929-1978, Archives of American Art, Smithsonian Institution, 1.
20 The Forrestals subsequently rented: *Register - New York County Abstract Index – U.S., W.P.A., Block 1361*, Section 5, 1-34; 000169, citation C7825, City of New York Department of Finance, Manhattan City Register.
20 During the Depression: Hoopes and Brinkley, 83; focusing...subjects: generally, Miles, compiled by Goodrich and Sterner, introduction.
21 Sterner's architectural aesthetic...precise craftsmanship: Miles, compiled by. Goodrich and Sterner, introduction. Sterner measured admired buildings while traveling in the United States and Europe and created finished drawings to promote awareness of them.
21 Sterner, who later...Museum of Modern Art: Miles, compiled by. "Record of Principal Work Executed by Harold Sterner."
21 Following a divorce...make a living: "Paula Trueman Wed to Harold Sterner," *NYT*, Nov. 18, 1935.
21 In 1946...to the location: Mary Roche, "Dilapidated Area Now Blooms Anew," *NYT*, May 24, 1946.

Renowned Residents of Beekman Place in the 1920s and '30s

32, 33 Sources: Miles, compiled by. Goodrich and Sterner, introduction; "Milestones, Nov. 22, 1943: Died. Colonel Van Santvoord Merle-Smith," *Time*, Nov. 22, 1943; Serge Obolensky, *One Man in His Time*, 20.; Gerard R. Wolfe, *New York: 15 Walking Tours Explore: An Architectural Guide to the Metropolis*, 362.; and, generally, *NYT* archives; Buddy Radisch, former Beekman Place Association president; Turtle Bay Association Web site, http://www.turtlebay-nyc.org/; U.S. Census, 1930, Enumeration District 614, Beekman Place.

Chapter Two: The Berlin Years, 1947-1989

Descriptions of furnishings and art work in 17 Beekman Place during the Berlin years, along with alterations to and social activities in the house, are from the author's conversations with Irving Berlin's three daughters—Mary Ellin Barrett, Linda Emmet, and Elizabeth Peters—from August to November 2009, and are not cited separately in the following notes.

39 It may have been the river's: Mary Ellin Barrett, conversation with author, Aug. 2009.
39 "Your father and I": Barrett conversation, Aug. 2009.
42 he often sneaked out of: *New York Sun*, Feb. 24, 1947.
42 got a job as a newsboy…Brooklyn and back: Woollcott, Alexander. *The Story of Irving Berlin*, 3-19.
42 "With me, as a kid": *New York Sun*, Feb. 24, 1947.
42 "It was in my blood": Freedland, Michael. *Irving Berlin*, 17.
42 sang and waited tables from: *New York Sun*, Feb. 24, 1947.
43 "The black keys are": *New York Press*, Dec. 20, 1914.
43 In Berlin's words, it set: Leopold, David. *Irving Berlin's Show Business*, 15.
44 "as poor as a family can be": Woollcott, 17.
44 buying his mother: Ibid., 16.
44 "all limp and sorry": Ibid., 103.
44 more than three hundred songs…ever written: Ibid., 225-237.
44 was selling faster than: Ibid., 148.
45 "Oh, Mr. Berlin,"…"use a little help": Barrett, Mary Ellin. *Irving Berlin: A Daughter's Memoir*, 21.
45 Soon, there were other: Ibid., 23.
45 distinctive six-story building: *New York Times (NYT)*, Oct. 15, 2006.
45 hired detectives to follow: Barrett, 30.
46 finally sent her off: Ibid., 31.
46 inspired by Ellin's absence: Ibid., 30.
46 moved Berlin to write: Ibid.
46 Ellin Mackay and Irving Berlin met: Ibid., 43.
47 Clarence Mackay, meanwhile: Ibid., 47.
47 Berlin presented her: Ibid., 48.
47 now redecorated to: Ibid., 53.
47 occasion for a new Berlin: Ibid., 55.
48 "We had more press": Kimball, Robert, and Linda Emmet. *The Complete Lyrics of Irving Berlin*, xix.
48 "There's no Lindy's": Barrett, 171. The original Lindy's opened in 1921, and a second in 1930. By 1969, both had closed. The present-day Lindy's has no connection to the originals. *NYT*, Sept. 9, 1969 and various.
48 "Even the sun is": Ibid., 137.
48 In 1930, Berlin and Ellin: Ibid., 87.
48 Instead, the Berlins moved: Kimball, xxiii.
49 "changing fashions": *Time*, May 28, 1934.
49 had to squelch suggestions: Leopold, 153.
49 "best show of a generation": *NYT*, July 5, 1942.
49 to scale back during: Linda Emmet, conversation with author, Aug. 2009.
50 Even before the war: Barrett conversation, Aug. 2009.
50 after a delay related to: Emmet conversation, Aug. 2009.
52 since it was delivered: David Kirkland, Steinway & Sons, interview with author, Nov. 25, 2009.
53 "When I started as a": *NYT*, May 11, 1966.
53 He said that even when: Jablonski, Edward. *Irving Berlin: American Troubadour*, 295.
53 Ellin asked a friend: Barrett conversation, Aug. 2009.
54 had been the subject of international: *NYT*, Mar. 24, 1884; Feb. 19, 1891; Sept. 6, 1928.
56 Five household staff…in charge: Barrett, Emmet conversations, Aug., Nov. 2009.
57 when she was twenty: Barrett, 101.
58 "It was a beautiful house, and": Anna Crouse, as told to Barrett, Aug. 2009.
59 Berlin and Ellin frequently: Barrett, Emmet conversations, Aug., Sept. 2009.
60 were raised "…not to be": Barrett, 122.

62 third woman ever to hold: *NYT*, June 22, 1949.
62 "An Oyster for Perle": *Time*, July 4, 1949.
62 "I've got a wonderful": Merman, Ethel. *Don't Call Me Madam*, 170.
63 "I love to write songs for": Thomas, Bob. *I Got Rhythm!: The Ethel Merman Story*, 112, 113.
63 "We weren't quite sure whether": Bergreen, Laurence. *As Thousands Cheer: The Life of Irving Berlin*, 500, from Archives of Performing Arts, University of Southern California, Los Angeles.
63 "It will star Ethel Merman": *Associated Press*, in *NYT*, Dec. 30, 1949.
63 "I was so upset": Mesta, Perle, with Robert Cahn. *Perle: My Story*, 155.
63 Weeks before its New York: Furia, Philip. *Irving Berlin: A Life in Song*, 247.
64 "There was a big hole": Jablonski, 267.
64 Crouse rushed into the theater: Abbott, George. *Mister Abbott*, 228.
64 "We'll never get offstage": Thomas, 111.
64 "most enchanting scores": *NYT*, Oct. 13, 1950.
65 "It is nice after all these years": Barrett, 262, citing Berlin correspondence with Harry Ruby.
65 "I was really flattered"…"talk about my play": Mesta, 163, 164.
66 "A publishing business in": Jablonski, 313, quoted from journalist Phyllis Battelle.
67 "I chased it all over the world": *Philadelphia Inquirer*, Aug. 26, 1966.
67 "She painted into that": Ibid.
67 He wrote a song to celebrate: Furia, 252.
67 Copyrighted but never published: Kimball, 464.
69 premiered as a benefit at the National: Jablonski, 300.
69 called for five encores: Furia, 261.
69 last known lyric less than: Emmet interview, *PBS*, Feb. 28, 2006.
69 "I'm a little farther uptown": *NYT*, May 11, 1966.
69 "I have nursed one idea": *Philadelphia Inquirer*, Aug. 26, 1966.
70 "Everything changed.": Barrett, 294, 295.
70 Berlin had taken up oil painting: Ibid., 273.
71 If he was happy with a portrait: Jablonski, 274.
71 "As a painter, I'm a": Ibid., 286.
71 In 1968, to mark his: *NYT*, May 6, 1968.
71 Later, Berlin and Ellin: Barrett conversation, Aug. 2009.
71 Ellin took her grandchildren: Barrett, 287.
71 Once, when his grandson: Barrett, 291.
71 His granddaughter Elizabeth: Ibid., 288.
72 "For a guy who keeps having birthdays": *NYT*, May 11, 1966.
72 "Turn on CBS": Barrett, 293.
72 "If I make it 'til then": Buddy Radisch, former Beekman Place Association president, interview with author, Aug. 2009.
72 One neighbor, cabaret singer: John Wallowitch, interview with author, Apr. 19, 2007.
73 stage of giant gold and silver: *NYT*, May 12, 1988.
73 honored guests sitting fourth row center: Barrett, 297.
73 Walter Cronkite opened the evening: Jablonski, 327.
73 The couple marked his one-hundredth: Barrett, 297.
74 On a mild December day four years later: *NYT*, Dec. 19, 1993.
74 …our history, our holidays, our homes, and our hearts: partial text of Walter Cronkite's tribute to Berlin on his one-hundredth birthday.

SIDEBARS

Berlin on Growing Up Poor

46 Irving Berlin returned to: *New York Sun*, Feb.24, 1947.
46 were packed into narrow tenement buildings: Jackson, Kenneth. *The Encyclopedia of New York City*, 696, 697.
46 "I'd get five and ten": *New York Sun*, Feb. 24, 1947.
46 "You never miss luxury": Ibid.
46 "Everyone should have": Bergreen, 8.

The Berlins and the Scouts

65 He and Ellin chose: Girl Scouts of the USA Archives, Ellin Berlin file.
65 To date, the trust fund: Irving Berlin Music Company on behalf of The God Bless America Fund.

Presidential Tributes

68 President Truman awarded Berlin: *NYT*, Oct. 2, 1945.

68 in a 1955 ceremony in Washington: *NYT*, Feb. 19, 1955.

68 And in 1977, President Ford: *NYT*, Jan. 2, 1977.

68 Instead, a representative of the president: Barrett conversation, Aug. 2009.

Chapter Three: The Luxembourg Years, 1990-Present

Unless noted, all factual information is based on printed source materials provided by the Luxembourg government and author's interviews with Luxembourg government personnel.

77 "We were all so pleased.": Mary Ellin Barrett, conversation with co-author, Hanlon, Aug. 2009.

78 "We did studies of several houses": Michel Franck, AIA, managing principal, Spacesmith; conversation with author, Jan. 2010.

78 "He called me back the next day": *New York Times (NYT)*, Dec. 13, 1993.

79 "It was an important project": Franck conversation, Jan. 2010.

79 They developed an innovative means: Ibid.

79 On the first floor, Berlin's projection booth: Ibid.

80 Major renovations were made on the third and fourth: Michel Franck, conversation with co-author Pickrel, Apr. 2005.

80 The windows and gates throughout the house: Franck conversation, Jan. 2010.

80 "We were very proud": Ibid.

85 In 963 AD, the first structure: Newcomer, James. *The Grand Duchy of Luxembourg*, 41.

86 A long line of Siegfried's descendants: Ibid., 55, 58.

86 In 1310, when he was just fourteen: Ibid., 85, 88.

86 "…he endowed his territory": Feis, René. *Cultural Guide to Luxembourg*, 79.

86 "Austria raised its flag over Luxembourg": Newcomer, 157.

86 In 1715, the country: Ibid., 157.

87 The country was designated a grand duchy: Ibid., 183.

88 "We are building bridges:" Ambassador Sylvie Lucas, permanent representative, Luxembourg Permanent Mission to the United Nations; conversation with author, Oct. 2009.

89 On World Food Day 2009: United Nations Web site (http://www.un.org/en/) (accessed Nov. 2009).

91 "The most severe global financial crisis: Lucas conversation, Oct. 2009.

91 "Going forward, we will continue to be proactive": Jean Olinger, deputy permanent representative, Luxembourg Permanent Mission to the United Nations; conversation with author, Mar. 2010.

92 "The Freedom Tower began to take shape": *NYT*, July 28, 2006.

92 "A mill doesn't exist in the U.S.": Ibid.

93 At its peak, Luxembourg was the seventh-largest": Skelton, Tim. *Luxembourg*, 8.

94 "As a representative of the TIO": François Knaff, executive director of the Trade and Investment Office; conversation with author, Sept. 2009.

96 "Both nations are positive, progressive, and": Ibid.

102 Recalling his summers as a child: Edward W. Emmet, conversation with author, Jan. 2010.

103 "Our goal is to encourage": Brigitte Goergen, director, Luxembourg National Tourist Office; conversation with author, Jan. 2010.

105 Designed by French architect: Christian de Portzamparc Web site (http://www.chdeportzamparc.com/) (accessed Jan. 2010).

106 Founded in 1987 by chef Paul Bocuse: Bocuse d'Or USA Web site (http://www.bocusedorusa.org/about.html) (accessed Jan. 2010).

106 "When we speak with": Goergen conversation, Feb. 2010.

107 "Hardly any other European capital city": Ibid.

110 "Our goal is to expedite the process": Saba Amroun-Febres, executive assistant to the consul general, Consulate General of Luxembourg; conversation with the author, Feb. 2010.

110 "While a strong economy is the backbone": Laurence Pierron, executive assistant to the executive director of the TIO, Trade and Investment Office; conversation with the author, Sept. 2009.

118 Written and directed by Ray Tostevin: Embassy

of Luxembourg in Washington Web site (http://washington.mae.lu/en) (accessed Jan. 2010).

120 "Irving Berlin was a remarkable man": artist Robert Hall; Nov. 20, 2009; event invitation; Arts at the Luxembourg House; Consulate General of Luxembourg, New York.

120 "Using the house as a place for cultural events": Edward W. Emmet conversation, Jan. 2010.

121 "...good luck came a-knocking at my door": "Blue Skies" (p. 121) by Irving Berlin; © Copyright 1926, 1927 by Irving Berlin; © Copyright Renewed. International Copyright Secured. All Rights Reserved. Reprinted by Permission of the Irving Berlin Music Company.

SIDEBARS

THE GIFT OF ART, THE ART OF PEACE

89 The legendary musician's tragic death: Permanent Mission of Luxembourg to the United Nations Web site (http://newyork-un.mae.lu/en) (accessed Nov. 2009).

89 The Luxembourg government acquired one: Ibid.

OUT-OF-THE-BOX THINKING

97 In a 1945 article, he explored the idea: The Arthur C. Clarke Foundation Web site (http://www.clarkefoundation.org/) (accessed Oct. 2009).

FLYING COLORS!

98 Cargolux, Luxembourg's largest freight carrier, is: Cargolux Web site (http://www.cargolux.lu/) (accessed Oct. 2009).

CELEBRATING ART, ARCHITECTURE AND AMERICANS

104 World-renowned architect I.M. Pei: MUDAM Luxembourg Web site (http://www.mudam.lu/en/accueil/) (accessed Oct. 2009).

EDWARD STEICHEN: THE GREAT CONNECTOR

108 The Family of Man debuted in 1955: Museum of Modern Art (MOMA) Web site (http://www.moma.org/) (accessed Nov. 2009).

BIBLIOGRAPHY

PROLOGUE: THE ELITE LEGACY OF BEEKMAN PLACE AND CHAPTER ONE: THE FORRESTAL YEARS, 1929-1946

BOOKS

Abbott, Carl. *Urban America in the Modern Age.* Arlington Heights, Ill.: Harlan Davidson, Inc., Arlington Heights, 1987.

Delaney, Edmund T. *New York's Turtle Bay, Old & New.* Barre, Mass.: Barre Publishers, 1965.

Ellis, Edward Robb. *The Epic of New York City: A Narrative History.* New York: Basic Books, 2004.

Feirstein, Sanna. *Naming New York: Manhattan Places & How They Got Their Names.* New York: New York University Press, 2001.

Gelernter, Mark. *A History of American Architecture: Buildings in Their Cultural and Technological Context.* Hanover, N.H.: University Press of New England, 1999.

Gerkens, Laurence. *The Shaping of the American City.* Hilliard, Oh.: The On-Call Faculty Program, Inc., 2002.

Goldstone, Harmon H. and Martha Dalrymple. *History Preserved: A Guide to New York City Landmarks and Historic Districts.* New York: Simon and Schuster, 1974.

Hanlon, Pamela. *Manhattan's Turtle Bay: Story of a Midtown Neighborhood.* Charleston, S.C.: Arcadia Publishing, 2008.

Harris, Cyril M., ed. Illustrated *Dictionary of Historic Architecture.* New York, Dover Publications Inc., 1977.

Hoopes, Townsend, and Douglas Brinkley. *Driven Patriot: The Life and Times of James Forrestal.* Annapolis: Naval Institute Press, 1992.

Hyde, Charles K. *The Dodge Brothers: The Men, the Motor Cars, and the Legacy.* Detroit: Wayne State University Press, 2005.

Jackson, Kenneth T., ed., *The Encyclopedia of New York City.* New Haven and London: Yale University Press, 1995.

Lockwood, Charles. Bricks and Brownstone: *The New York Row House, 1783-1929* New York: Rizzoli International Publications, 2003.

Macpherson, John. *Epidemic Cholera: Its Mission and Mystery, Haunts and Havocs, Pathology and Treatments.* New York: Carleton, 1866.

Obolensky, Serge. *One Man in His Time.* New York: Mc Dowell, 1958.

Patterson, Jerry E. *Fifth Avenue: The Best Address.* New York: Rizzoli International Publications, Inc., 1998.

Rogow, Arnold A., *James Forrestal: A Study of Personality, Politics and Policy.* New York: The Macmillan Company, 1963.

Stern, Robert A.M., Gregory Gilmartin, and Thomas Mellins. *New York 1930: Architecture and Urbanism Between the Two World Wars.* New York: Rizzoli International Publications, 1987.

von Pressentin Wright, Carol. *Blue Guide: New York.* London: A&C Black Limited; New York: W.W. Norton & Company, Inc., Second Edition, 1991.

White, Philip L. *The Beekmans of New York in Politics and Commerce, 1647-1877.* Baltimore: The New-Historical Society, printed by the Waverly Press, 1956.

Wolfe, Gerard R. *New York: 15 Walking Tours Explore: An Architectural Guide to the Metropolis.* New York: The McGraw-Hill Companies, 2003.

Zaitzevsky, Cynthia. *Long Island Landscapes and the Women Who Designed Them.* New York: W. W. Norton & Company, Inc., 2009.

PERIODICALS AND OTHER

Miles, Christine M., compiled by. *Harold Sterner: Architect & Artist, A Retrospective of His Work – April 1-June 15, 1978* (Washington, D.C., The American Institute of Architects Foundation, 1978), exhibition catalog.

New York Times

Oculus (quarterly magazine of the American Institute of Architects' New York Chapter)

Time

WEB SITES

Arlington National Cemetery
Beekman Place Apartments
New York Building Information System
New York Public Library Digital Gallery
Princeton Forrestal Center
Princeton University
The Turtle Bay Association

CHAPTER TWO: THE BERLIN YEARS, 1947-1989

BOOKS

Abbott, George. *Mister Abbott.* New York: Random House, 1963.

Anderson, Alan. *The Songwriter Goes to War: The Story of Irving Berlin's World War II All-Army Production of This Is the Army*. Pompton Plains, N.J.: Amadeus Press/Limelight Editions, 2004.

Barrett, Mary Ellin. *Irving Berlin: A Daughter's Memoir.* New York: Simon & Schuster, 1994.

Berlin, Ellin. *Silver Platter: A Portrait of Mrs. John Mackay*. Garden City, N.Y.: Doubleday & Company, 1957.

Bergreen, Laurence. *As Thousands Cheer: The Life of Irving Berlin.* New York: Viking, 1990.

Kimball, Robert, and Linda Emmet. *The Complete Lyrics of Irving Berlin.* New York: Alfred A. Knopf, 2001.

Furia, Philip. *Irving Berlin: A Life in Song.* New York: Schirmer Books, 1998.

Freedland, Michael. *Irving Berlin.* New York: Stein and Day, 1974.

Jablonski, Edward. *Irving Berlin: American Troubadour.* New York: Henry Holt, 1999.

Jackson, Kenneth., ed. *The Encyclopedia of New York City*. New Haven and London: Yale University Press, 1995.

Leopold, David. *Irving Berlin's Show Business.* New York: Harry N. Abrams, 2005.

Lesch, Paul. *Playing her Part: Perle Mesta in Luxembourg*. Luxembourg: American Chamber of Commerce in Luxembourg, 2001.

Mesta, Perle, with Robert Cahn. *Perle: My Story.* New York: McGraw Hill, 1960.

Merman, Ethel. *Don't Call Me Madam*. London: W.H. Allen, 1955.

Rosen, Jody. *White Christmas. The Story of an*

American Song. New York: Scribner, 2002.
Thomas, Bob. *I Got Rhythm!: The Ethel Merman Story*. New York: Putnam's Sons, 1985.
Wilson, Richard Guy. *Harbor Hill: Portrait of a House*. New York: W.W. Norton & Co., 2008.
Woollcott, Alexander. *The Story of Irving Berlin*. New York: G.P. Putnam's Sons, 1925.

PERIODICALS AND OTHER:

New York Daily News
New York Sun
New York Times
New York Press
Philadelphia Inquirer
Time

Girl Scouts of the USA Archives
Irving Berlin Music Company
Steinway & Sons
Public Broadcasting System

Chapter Three: The Luxembourg Years, 1990-Present

BOOKS

Feis, René (and multiple authors). *Cultural Guide to Luxembourg*. Government of Luxembourg: Under the patronage of the Ministry of Culture, Higher Education and Research, 2005.
Newcomer, James. *The Grand Duchy of Luxembourg*. Lanham, Maryland: University Press of America, Inc., 1984
Skelton, Tim. *Luxembourg*. England: Bradt Travel Guide Ltd, 2008.

PERIODICALS AND OTHER

New York Times
Letter to Consul General Thein from Governor Mario M. Cuomo

WEB SITES

Bocuse d'Or USA
Cargolux
Christian de Portzamparc
Consulate General of Luxembourg in New York
Embassy of Luxembourg in Washington
Luxembourg American Chamber of Commerce
Luxembourg National Tourist Office
MUDAM Luxembourg
Permanent Mission of Luxembourg to the United Nations
The Arthur C. Clarke Foundation
The Museum of Modern Art (MOMA)
United Nations

Credits

COVER PHOTOGRAPHS

© Marc Weydert

IMAGES

Denoted by page and position: t = top, b = bottom, l = left, r = right, ul = upper left, ur – upper right, uc = upper center, ll = lower left, lr – lower right, lc = lower center, cr = center right, cl = center left, bkgr = background.

Prologue: The Elite Legacy of Beekman Place

Collection of The New-York Historical Society: 82924d, 6; 76943d, 8; and 76861d, 9; Office for Metropolitan History: 10t; Milstein Division of United States History, Local History & Geneaology, The New York Public Library, Astor, Lenox and Tilden Foundations: 10b; Courtesy of N. Streeter: 11.

Chapter One: The Forrestal Years, 1929-1946

FLOOR PLANS

Floor plans of 17 Beekman Place, 1932, were developed by Terry Hudak, based on the original design by Harold Sterner.

IMAGES

Courtesy of: ©Yousuf Karsh, 1945:m12; ©Underwood & Underwood/Corbis: 14; ©Bettmann/Corbis: 15; the Forrestal family: 16, 18 (Cecil Beaton, photographer), 31; Arnold Genthe Collection, Prints & Photographs Division, Library of Congress, LC-G412-T-5122-002: 20; Museum of the City of New York, Wurts Brothers

Collection: 22; 69917 Collection of The New-York Historical Society: 23ul; Author: 23ur, 25b, 28ul; The Luxembourg House, New York, 24t, 24b, 28t, 30; The Harold Sterner Papers, 1929-1978, Archives of American Art, Smithsonian Institution: 25t, 26, 27, 28b, 29; Kathy McGilvery: 33; Millicent Ogden McKinley Cox: 34; ©AP Images: 35.

Chapter Two: The Berlin Years, 1947-1989

IMAGES

Courtesy of Rodgers & Hammerstein: An Imagem Company, on behalf of the Estate of Irving Berlin: 38, 43, 44, and sheet music covers, 40, 50, 62, 67; Courtesy Photofest: 42, 48, 49, 63, 64, 68, 69; Private Collection: 45, 56, 57, 58, 65, 73 (56, 57, also courtesy of David Leopold, author of *Irving Berlin's Show Business*); *New York Daily News*, 47; "Photographs-Fullerton" by Henry S. Fullerton, 3rd, from *The Finest Rooms by America's Great Decorators*, edited by Katherine Tweed, copyright © 1964 by The Viking Press. Used by permission of Viking Penguin, a division of Penguin Group (USA) Inc., 52, 54-55; © Bruce Davidson/Magnum Photos, 60; Marc Weydert, 74.

SONG LYRICS

The following lyrics are reprinted by permission of the Irving Berlin Music Company:

"All Alone" (p. 46) by Irving Berlin; ©Copyright 1924 by Irving Berlin; ©Copyright Renewed. International Copyright Secured. All Rights Reserved. Reprinted by Permission.

"Remember" (p. 46) by Irving Berlin; ©Copyright 1925 by Irving Berlin; ©Copyright Renewed. International Copyright Secured. All Rights Reserved. Reprinted by Permission.

"Always" (p. 46) by Irving Berlin; ©Copyright 1925 by Irving Berlin; ©Copyright Renewed. International Copyright Secured. All Rights Reserved. Reprinted by Permission.

"Blue Skies" (p. 47) by Irving Berlin; ©Copyright 1926, 1927 by Irving Berlin; ©Copyright Renewed. International Copyright Secured. All Rights Reserved. Reprinted by Permission.

"You're Just In Love" (p.64) by Irving Berlin; ©Copyright 1950 by Irving Berlin; ©Copyright Renewed. International Copyright Secured. All Rights Reserved. Reprinted by Permission.

"Silver Platter" (p. 67-68) by Irving Berlin; ©Copyright 1957 by Irving Berlin;©Copyright Renewed. International Copyright Secured. All Rights Reserved. Reprinted by Permission.

Chapter Three: The Luxembourg Years, 1990-Present

IMAGES

Courtesy of: ©Marc Weydert: 76, 80cl, 80ll, 82, 83, 89ll, 90ll, 110, 115lr; The Luxembourg House, New York: 78, 79 (both), 80ul, 81, 84, 87lr, 88ul, 91ur, 92 (both), 93, 95ll, 98, 99 (both), 100, 101, 102, 107cr, 108ll (photograph by Edward Steichen, gift of Joanna T. Steichen), 109 (all), 111 (both), 112ul, 113 (both), 114 (both), 115ur, 116 ul, 119 (both), 120ll, 121 (both), 122; Luxembourg Office National du Tourisme (ONT): 85, 86, 87ur, 94, 95ur, 103ur, 104, 105 (both), 108ul; The United Nations: 88ll = ©2010 UN Photo/Mark Garten, 89ur = ©2009 UN Photo/Evan Schneider; Luxembourg Service Information et Presse (SIP): 90ul (©Charles Caratini, 2009); ArcelorMittal: 91lr; Michael Anton: 97ur; SES: 97cr; Wade Zimmerman: 103lr; Luxembourg Ministère des Classes Moyennes et du Tourisme, Département du Tourisme: 106ll, 107ur; Marc Theis: 106ul; Ernie Hammes: 112cl; Sébastien Grébille: 112ll; Vicky Hinger: 116ll; Véronique Rischard: 117ur; Centre National de l'Audiovisuel (CNA) and Samsa Film: 117lr; CNA: 118ul; Tanya Majerus: 118cl; CNA and Grace Productions: 118ll; David Leopold, author of Irving Berlin's Show Business (New York; Harry N. Abrams, Incorporated; 2005): 120ul.

SONG LYRICS

"Blue Skies" (p. 121), by Irving Berlin; ©Copyright 1926, 1927 by Irving Berlin; ©Copyright Renewed. International Copyright Secured. All Rights Reserved. Reprinted by Permission of the Irving Berlin Music Company.

The authors have made all reasonable efforts to find and secure permissions and reproduction rights. Any omissions or errors are inadvertent.

AUTHOR PHOTOGRAPHS
Debra Pickrel: ©Jennifer Calais Smith
Marianne Matthews: ©Kristin Kysiak Hoebermann; Hoebermann Studio, Inc.

Author Biographies

Debra Pickrel, a communications and marketing executive, is co-author of *Frank Lloyd Wright in New York: The Plaza Years, 1954-1959*, recipient of the 2008 Independent Publishers Book Awards' Gold Medal in Architecture. She has written for *Architectural Record, House Beautiful, Metropolis*, and *Preservation*, and also penned *A Day in Turtle Bay*, a walking tour of her Manhattan neighborhood. A journalism graduate of the University of North Carolina at Chapel Hill, she received her MA in historic preservation from Goucher College.

Pamela Hanlon, a writer and communications consultant, formerly was vice president-public relations for American Express Company. During a more than thirty-five-year career in communications, she also held senior positions with United Airlines, ITT Corporation, and Pan American World Airways. A graduate of the University of Missouri Journalism School, Hanlon began her career as a reporter for the Associated Press. She is author of *Manhattan's Turtle Bay: Story of a Midtown Neighborhood*, published in 2008.

Marianne Matthews is a business, editorial, and creative writer. Her marketing-communications experience spans twenty-five years, writing and producing projects for corporations such as Schering-Plough, Con Edison, and Oppenheimer Management. She has had over twenty-five articles published in trade magazines and is presently editor of *Imaging Economics*, a business journal for physicians. Marianne is also an actress and a produced playwright. She holds an MA in English from New York University and an MFA in acting from The Actors Studio Drama School at New School University.